EXCITED DELIRIUM SYNDROME

Cause of Death and Prevention

EXCITED DELIRIUM SYNDROME

Cause of Death and Prevention

Theresa G. Di Maio
Vincent J.M. Di Maio

Taylor & Francis
Taylor & Francis Group

Boca Raton   London   New York

A CRC title, part of the Taylor & Francis imprint, a member of the
Taylor & Francis Group, the academic division of T&F Informa plc.

Published in 2006 by
CRC Press
Taylor & Francis Group
6000 Broken Sound Parkway NW, Suite 300
Boca Raton, FL 33487-2742

International Standard Book Number-10: 0-8493-1611-1 (Hardcover)
International Standard Book Number-13: 978-0-8493-1611-1 (Hardcover)
Library of Congress Card Number 2005049423

Library of Congress Cataloging-in-Publication Data

Di Maio, Theresa.
    Excited delirium syndrome : cause of death and prevention / Theresa DiMaio, Vincent J.M. DiMaio.
        p. ; cm.
    Includes bibliographical references and index.
    ISBN 0-8493-1611-1 (alk. paper)
    1. Excited delirium syndrome. 2. Prisoners--Death. 3. Mentally ill--Death. I. Di Maio, Vincent J. M., 1941- II. Title.
    [DNLM: 1. Delirium--diganosis. 2. Psychoses, Substance-Induced--diagnosis. 3. Death, Sudden, Cardiac--etiology. 4. Delerium--prevention & control. 5. Mentally Ill Persons. 6. Restraint, Physical. WM 220 D5347e 2005]

RC520.7.D56 2005
616.89--dc22
                                                  2005049423

Taylor & Francis Group
is the Academic Division of T&F Informa plc.

Visit the Taylor & Francis Web site at
http://www.taylorandfrancis.com

and the CRC Press Web site at
http://www.crcpress.com

DEDICATION

This book is dedicated to all law enforcement and medical personnel who have been wrongfully accused of misconduct in deaths due to excited delirium syndrome.

PREFACE

Beginning in the early 1980s, an increasing number of deaths in association with excited delirium and physical restraint by law enforcement personnel occurred. This has continued to the present time. Most of these deaths are associated with abuse of cocaine or methamphetamine. At the same time, a smaller number of deaths, unrelated to cocaine and methamphetamine abuse, were reported in mental institutions. These deaths, which occurred while in police custody or in mental institutions, were nearly universally blamed on the actions of police and medical personnel attempting physical restraint. Numerous lawsuits were filed and in some cases criminal prosecution was either instituted or proposed.

The senior author of this book (T.G.D.) obtained her Bachelor of Nursing degree from the School of Nursing at the University of Texas Health Science at San Antonio. Following this, she worked as a psychiatric nurse. It was at this time that she encountered and responded to numerous individuals experiencing acute psychotic episodes requiring physical restraint. This led to an interest in the cause of sudden death in acutely psychotic patients in psychiatric settings and, thus, the genesis of this book. While writing this book, she obtained a Graduate Certificate in Forensic Nursing from Beth-El College of Nursing and Health Sciences of the University of Colorado at Colorado Springs. She has lectured to nurses, police, and the general scientific community on excited delirium syndrome.

The second author (V.J.M.D.) is a forensic pathologist with 35 years experience in the field. He is the Chief Medical Examiner of Bexar County Texas, Professor in the Department of Pathology at the University of Texas Health Science at San Antonio, Editor of the *American Journal of Medicine and Pathology*, and the author of three texts on forensic pathology. His interest in the excited delirium syndrome was initiated by the senior author.

It is hoped that this book will dispel some of the misconceptions regarding deaths due to excited delirium syndrome, present a rational explanation for this entity, and present ways that deaths from excited delirium can be prevented.

ACKNOWLEDGMENTS

The writing of this book could not have been accomplished without the encouragement, support, and unwavering love of my husband, Dr. Vincent J.M. Di Maio, who has always believed in me and my vision for this book. Without his encouragement and contribution to this text, it would not have been possible for me, a first time author, to bring this study and explanation of this unique death syndrome to publication.

I wish to express my gratitude to Virginia Lynch, a friend and visionary in Forensic Nursing. She was responsible for opening the door in my life to the field of Forensic Nursing. Her continued encouragement and friendship has helped guide me through the writing of this book.

I would also like to thank Becky McEldowney Masterman, of CRC Press, for encouraging me to write this book and Dr. Suzanna E. Dana, a friend, for aid with the illustrations.

Though only her spirit is here with me to share in my success, I must thank my mother, a nurse, who always dreamed for me.

Lastly, I thank the Lord, our God, who orchestrates our lives.

ABOUT THE AUTHORS

Theresa G. Di Maio, BFA, BSN, RN, FN

Vincent J.M. Di Maio, M.D.
Chief Medical Examiner, Bexar County, TX
Professor, Department of Pathology
University of Texas Health Science Center–San Antonio

CONTENTS

1

INTRODUCTION TO DEATH DUE TO EXCITED DELIRIUM SYNDROME

"It is truly a mark of strength, however, to be willing to admit that we have things to learn."

— Shakti Gawain
(from Paulo Coelho,
The Alchemist: A Fable About Following Your Dream)

Excited delirium syndrome involves the sudden death of an individual, during or following an episode of excited delirium, in which an autopsy fails to reveal evidence of sufficient trauma or natural disease to explain the death. In virtually all such cases, the episode of excited delirium is terminated by a struggle with police or medical personnel, and the use of physical restraint. Typically, within a few to several minutes following cessation of the struggle, the individual is noted to be in cardiopulmonary arrest. Attempts at resuscitation are usually unsuccessful. If resuscitation is "successful," the individual is found to have suffered irreversible hypoxic encephalopathy and death occurs in a matter of days.

Delirium involves an acute (minutes to hours), transient disturbance in consciousness and cognition.[1] There is disorientation; disorganized and inconsistent thought processes; inability to distinguish reality from hallucinations; disturbances in speech; disorientation to time and place; misidentification of individuals. When the delirium involves combative and/or violent behavior, it is termed **excited delirium**. Delirium should not be confused with **dementia,** which involves a progressive mental deterioration due to organic factors, e.g. Alzheimer's disease. In dementia, the symptoms are chronic and involve global impairment of intellectual function.

The concept of death due to excited delirium was introduced by Dr Luther Bell in 1849.[2] Dr. Bell thought that he was describing a new disease,

1

a fatal form of delirium in the mentally ill. Typically, patients presented with fever, a rapid pulse, a lack of appetite and sleep. They were agitated and anxious, with increasing confusion that appeared suddenly. Any attempt to approach the patient resulted in a violent struggle. Typically, the patient continued to deteriorate over a course of weeks before dying. Deaths due to Bell's mania continued to be reported in the medical literature until the early 1950s when they abruptly disappeared. This coincided with the introduction of pheothiazines for treatment of mental illness.[3–4]

While all of Bell's patients had mental disease, and symptoms of excited delirium present for days to weeks prior to death, deaths seen today in association with excited delirium mainly involve abusers of stimulants, e.g., cocaine, methamphetamine, with symptoms present for only hours. Less commonly, deaths occur without the presence of these drugs in individuals with endogenous mental disease. Thus, Bell's mania represents a chronic form of fatal excited delirium different in clinical presentation and mechanism of death from current cases of death due to excited delirium.

The mechanism of death in the modern version of Bell's mania is controversial. Since such deaths almost always occur after restraint is either instituted or attempted, the cause of death is often attributed to the application of a "choke hold" or "restraint/positional asphyxia," even when there is neither testimonial nor physical evidence of these.[5–11] In deaths involving excited delirium in which hog-tie restraint has been used (a common method of restraint used by police in arresting violent individuals), it was alleged that death was due to positional asphyxia.[6–11] Because of the circumstances surrounding deaths due to excited delirium, there are often charges of police or medical misconduct. In some cases, allegations of murder are made. When no physical cause for the death is found at autopsy, this is ascribed to a cover-up.

The initial reports on deaths due to the modern form of excited delirium focused on the development of hyperthermia in these individuals.[12] In practice, this is frequently absent or at least not noted. One of the problems is that while virtually all individuals dying of excited delirium syndrome are transported to hospitals in an attempt to resuscitate them, Emergency Room personnel often do not take temperatures, or if they do, do not record them. By the time the medical examiner's office gets the case, the body has either been refrigerated or left in an air-conditioned room for a number of hours.

In deaths due to excited delirium syndrome, an autopsy fails to reveal evidence of sufficient trauma or natural disease to explain the death. In regard to trauma, the usual findings are minor abrasions and contusions explainable by the struggle that preceded death. If during the struggle the individual was either hit in the neck or an arm placed around it, hemorrhage in the neck may be present. In rare instances fractures of the superior horns of the thyroid cartilage or the hyoid bone occur. This leads some individuals to contend that manual strangulation has occurred. What they fail to realize is that both hemorrhage in the neck and the aforementioned fractures do not equate to death due to strangulation. They are only *markers* indicating that pressure or a blow to the neck has occurred.[13] The aforementioned injuries are not in themselves lethal. Death from manual strangulation involves constant pressure to the neck over a number of minutes — generally more than 2 minutes.

Farnham and Kennedy[14] feel that there is a problem with the perception of death due to excited delirium by the legal system, the public and the press. The problem is that legal "reasoning favors single proximate causes rather than medical conditions, but the intervention most proximate to the time of death is not necessarily the cause of death." Karch pointed out the same problem, a tendency to confuse proximity of an action, e.g., hog-tying, with causality, an error in logic identified by Aristotle more than 2300 years ago.[15] "Compounding the situation is that popular journalism favors controversy and blame rather than balance and exploration."[14]

Most individuals succumbing to excited delirium syndrome are under the influence of illegal stimulants and die during or immediately after their arrest. Karch and Stephens[16] divided drug-related deaths in prisoners into four categories: those occurring (1) during arrest and transport, (2) within 24 hours of arrest, (3) after 24 hours but before trial, and (4) after trial. They stated, "Excited delirium in chronic stimulant abusers is the principal cause of death during arrest and transport."[16] They felt that, in these cases, while survival is theoretically possible, given the ineffectiveness of current methods of treatment, "it is not likely."[16]

The two stimulants most commonly associated with death due to excited delirium syndrome are cocaine and methamphetamine. Rarely, the drug of abuse is phencyclidine (PCP). The rarity of the latter cases may be due to its infrequent use nationwide. Even rarer are deaths seen in association with acute and chronic alcoholism.[13]

High blood concentrations of cocaine cannot in themselves be the mechanism of death in excited delirium syndrome, as the concentrations of cocaine in these cases is similar to those in asymptomatic recreational users.[12,17,18] In fact, deaths attributed to cocaine, whether they are or are not associated with excited delirium syndrome, have cocaine levels in the blood that overlap those using cocaine but who die of trauma with cocaine an incidental finding.[17,18] There is also no correlation between death and levels of methamphetamine in the blood.[19]

Less commonly, deaths related to excited delirium syndrome occur in individuals with organic mental disease who are not using drugs of abuse.[9-11] In these cases, death may occur not only during attempts to arrest the individuals but also in mental institutions when medical personnel attempt to restrain an individual for violent behavior.

In individuals with intrinsic mental disease, death usually occurs following institution of restraint because of an acute psychotic episode. An **acute psychotic episode** (APE) is characterized by abrupt disturbance of thought, behavior, and mood. It may be an acute event or an exacerbation of an underlying chronic condition. Agitation and violence are not necessarily a part of APE but individuals experiencing it are always at risk for these. An APE may be due to intrinsic mental disease, a medical condition, or a drug. Acute psychotic episodes are common in schizophrenia, schizo-affective disorders, severe mood disorders, and delusional disorders. For all practical purposes an acute psychotic episode with agitation and violence is synonymous with excited delirium.

Deaths occurring in psychiatric patients not on illegal stimulants may be associated with underlying natural disease and/or the presence of psychotropic drugs. Many of these drugs are cardiotoxic with some having effects on the cardiovascular system similar to cocaine.[20-23] Just as with excited delirium syndrome due to use of illegal stimulants, if a patient becomes violent, steps must be taken to protect the safety of both the patient and others. If all nonphysical methods are utilized without avail, then medical personnel have to resort to use of physical restraints. If death occurs, members of the public, as well as physicians inexperienced in the handling of patients experiencing an acute psychotic episode, will often then proclaim that the patient has been brutalized by the health-care workers.

The problem with excited delirium syndrome is that the interpretation of such deaths has been handled with an underlying assumption: if the death occurred, it had to be due to misconduct by police and/or medical personnel. That death can be due to the normal physiological reactions of the body to stress gone awry, and to the use of stimulants, does not conform to the present mind-set of many Americans, that anytime tragedy occurs someone must be at fault and they should be punished, or even better, sued.

REFERENCES

1. American Psychiatric Association. *Diagnostic and Statistical Manual of Mental Disorders*, 4th ed., text revision. American Psychiatric Association, Washington, D.C., 2000.
2. Bell, L.V. On a form of disease resembling some advanced stages of mania and fever. *Am. J. Insanity* 6:97–127, 1849.
3. Cancro, R. The introduction of neuroleptics: a psychiatric revolution. *Psychiatr. Serv.* 51(3), 333–335, 2000.

4. Lieberman, J.A., Golden, R., Stroup, S., and McEnvoy, J. Drugs of the psychopharmacological revolution in clinical psychiatry. *Psychiatr. Serv.* 51(10):1254–1258, 2000.

5. Reay, D.T. and Eisele, J.W. Death from law enforcement neck holds. *Am. J Forensic Med. Pathol.* 3(3):253–258, 1982.

6. Stratton, S.J., Rogers, C., and Green, K. Sudden death in individuals in hobble restraints during paramedic transport. *Ann. Emerg. Med.* 25(5):710–712, 1995.

7. Reay, D.T., Howard, J.D., Fligner, C.L., and Ward, R.J. Effects of positional restraint on oxygen saturation and heart rate following exercise. *Am J. Forensic Med. Pathol.* 9(1):16–18, 1988.

8. Reay, D.T., Fligner, C.L., Stilwell, A.D., and Arnold J. Positional asphyxia during law enforcement transport. *Am. J. Forensic Med. Pathol.* 13(2):90–97, 1992.

9. O'Halloran, R.L. and Lewman, L.V. Restraint asphyxiation in excited delirium. *Am. J. Forensic Med. Pathol.* 14(4):289–295, 1993.

10. O'Halloran, R.L. and Frank, J.G. Asphyxial death during prone restraint position revisited: a report of 21 cases. *Am. J. Forensic Med. Pathol.* 21(1):39–52, 2000.

11. Pollanen, M., Chiasson, D.A., and Cairns, J.T. Unexpected death related to restraint for excited delirium: a retrospective study of deaths in police custody and in the community. *Can. Med. Assoc. J.* 158(12):1603–1607, 1998.

12. Wetli, C.V., Mash, D., and Karch, S.B. Cocaine-associated agitated delirium and the neuroleptic malignant syndrome. *Am. J Emerg. Med.* 14(4):425–428, 1996.

13. Di Maio, V.J.M. and Di Maio, D.J. *Forensic Pathology,* 2nd ed. CRC Press, Boca Raton, FL, 2001.

14. Farnham, F.R. and Kennedy, H.G. Acute excited states and sudden death: much journalism, little evidence. *Br. Med. J.* 315(7116):1107–1108, 1997.

15. Karch, S.B. *Karch's Pathology of Drug Abuse.* CRC Press, Boca Raton, FL, 2002.

16. Karch, S.B. and Stephens, B. Drug abusers who die during arrest or in custody. *J. R. Soc. Med.* 92(3):110–113, 1999.

17. Karch, S.B. and Stephens, B.G. Acute excited states and sudden death; acute excited states are not caused by high blood concentrations of cocaine. *Br. Med. J.* 316(7138):1171, 1998.

18. Karch, S.B., Stephens, B.G., and Ho, C.H. Relating cocaine blood concentrations to toxicity: an autopsy study of 99 cases. *J. Forensic Sci.* 43(1):41–45, 1998.

19. Karch, S.B., Stephens, B.G., and Ho, C.H. Methamphetamine related deaths in San Francisco: demographic, pathologic and toxicologic profiles. *J Forensic Sci.* 44(2):359–368, 1999.

20. Roden, D.M. Drug-induced prolongation of the QT interval. *N. Engl. J. Med.* 350:1013–1022, 2004.

21. Herxheimer, A. Arrhythmias and sudden death in patients taking antipsychotic drugs. *Br. Med. J.* 325:1253–1254, 2002.

22. Fayek, M., Kingsbury, S.J., Zada, J., and Simpson, G.M. Psychopharmacology: cardiac effects of antipsychotic medications. *Psychiatr. Serv.* 52:607–609, 2001.

23. Witchel, H., Hancox, J.C., and Nutt, D.J. Psychotropic drugs, cardiac arrhythmia, and sudden death. *J. Clin. Psychopharmacol.* 23(1):58–77, 2003.

2

HISTORY OF EXCITED DELIRIUM SYNDROME

Sudden death in association with excited delirium (the excited delirium syndrome) is a unique phenomenon, currently primarily associated with the abuse of illegal stimulant drugs. Reports of such deaths began to appear in the medical literature in the early 1980s.[1,2] Prior to this time, death in association with excited delirium was associated with endogenous mental disease and had a chronic course with symptoms presenting over weeks to months. This chronic entity, originally described by Dr. Luther Bell in 1849, seemed to "disappear" during the 1950s.[3,4] Present-day deaths, occurring in either stimulant abusers or psychiatric patients, are of the acute, sudden-death form, with death occurring minutes to hours after development of excited delirium and in which there is usually use of physical restraint. It is this *acute* or sudden form of death that is the concern of this book. In discussing the causality of present-day deaths, we must first, however, explore the historical antecedents of this entity.

BELL'S MANIA

The first reports of death in association with excited delirium appear in the psychiatric literature in the mid and late 19th century in both the United States and Europe and involve patients in mental facilities. This entity was given various names: acute exhaustive mania, Bell's mania, fatal catatonia, acute exhaustive psychosis, etc.[4] All of these deaths had one notable feature; they defied all known causation.

The first report in the American medical literature was in 1849 by Dr. Luther V. Bell, a physician and superintendent at the McLean Asylum for the Insane, in Sommerville, Massachusetts.[3] Dr. Bell described the symptoms of what he believed to be a new disease among the mentally ill inpatients of this asylum. This "new disease" would come to be known as "Bell's mania."

Dr. Bell noticed that a number of patients were dying unexpectedly from unknown causes. He concluded that he was witnessing a new form of a disease — a unique form of death in a particular subgroup of psychiatric patients.

> That a new disease would be manifested at this advanced day, in the calendar of medical history, is not without many precedents. That such should occur in the great family of maladies involving the nervous system, would be the least improbable, when we reflect how less than all others these have been studied, comprehended and treated, until within a comparatively recent period.[3]

From December of 1836 to January 1849, over a period of 12 years and 1700 admissions, Dr. Bell identified 40 cases of excited delirium, in three-quarters of which the patient would die from this previously unknown lethal physiological state.

> On the other hand, if the tendency is favorable, convalesce is established in about the same period, and the sufferer emerges in a state of absolute recovery at once, as he would do in the delirium of any acute disease.[3]

Bell goes on to state that there are no residual impairments of mental integrity and the cure is permanent.

Bell depicted a state in which the patient's overall health deteriorates dramatically, progressing into a lethal, downward-spiraling physiological course with death occurring in 2 or 3 weeks. The clinical symptoms described by Dr. Bell were as follows:

> Acute onset of symptoms
> Mania
> Violent behavior
> Need for restraint
> Refusal of food
> Inability to sleep
> Fatigue deteriorating to exhaustion and circulatory collapse

> The progress of the disease does not present any great change of characteristics. The patient will get so little food, so little

sleep and be exercised with such constant restlessness and anxiety, that he will fall off from day to day. The emaciation goes on with rapidity unexampled in the cases of mania, or fever, or delirium tremens. At the expiration of two to three weeks, your patient will sink in death, diarrhea occasionally supervening a few days previously.[5]

Death in Bell's patients and most patients dying of the chronic form of excited delirium was probably due to a combination of electrolyte disturbances, dehydration, and chronic catecholamine insult on the cardiovascular system. Other contributory factors, such as intervening infections and unusual treatment modalities, cannot be dismissed, however.

In Europe in the late 19th century, Dr. Emil Kraepelin, a German psychiatrist, developed a classification of mental illness based on symptoms, causes, and course. Utilization of this classification results in the ability to identify particular subgroups of patients that are at high risk for sudden death due to excited delirium syndrome. Kraepelin drew a distinction between manic–depressive psychosis and dementia praecox, now called schizophrenia.[5] In Kraepelin's published works on dementia praecox, his discussion on the mortality of this particular subgroup of mentally ill individuals is of interest:[5]

> But lastly, in certain circumstances the morbid process as such may also lead to death. Occasionally, though seldom, it is observed that in severe states of excitement of long duration a steadily progressive loss of strength gradually makes its appearance, which continues even when the patients become quieter and take abundant nourishment. Finally death ensues with extreme cardiac weakness and great sinking of the temperature without the autopsy showing any perceptible organic disease at all.
>
> Less uncertain is the causation of death by the morbid process itself in those somewhat frequent cases, in which the death of the patients results at the height of severe excitement, accompanied by phenomena of cerebral irritation with convulsions or paralyses, sometimes with almost continuous seizures.

Thus, across continents, and half a century, both Dr. Bell in the United States and Dr. Kraepelin, in Munich, were documenting a unique and fatal syndrome involving excited delirium. The symptoms and signs of this entity usually presented over weeks and months and resulted in both mental and physical deterioration. Thus, their syndrome was of a chronic nature. What we are seeing today is an acute presentation with death occurring minutes or hours after onset of symptoms rather than after weeks of prolonged mental and physiological deterioration.

In 1933, Dr. Irving M. Derby, a pathologist at Brooklyn State Hospital in New York, described 148 deaths from what he called "manic–depressive exhaustion," an entity that was called by others acute delirium, acute dementia praecox, catatonic death, or Bell's mania.[6]

Brooklyn State Hospital was known for admitting acutely disturbed and violent patients. Dr. Derby noticed that an unusually high percentage of "manic–depressive" patients were dying from "exhaustion." During a 5-year period from 1927 to 1932, a total of 386 manic–depressive patients died. Of this group, 187 (48%) died with accompanying exhaustion and excitement. Analysis of these cases revealed that in 148 instances death was attributable to exhaustion. This group consisted of 139 females and 9 men. The predominance of females is unexplained. The ages of the patients ranged from 17 to 63 years, with 87 deaths in individuals from 17 through 35 years of age; 48 in individuals 36 to 50, and 13 individuals older than 50 years of age. This preponderance of young individuals is consistent with what we see today.

Of the 148 patients whose deaths were attributed to exhaustion, 82 patients (55%) were considered acute cases with less than 1 week in residence in the hospital. This statistic is deceptive, however, as most patients had symptoms for a number of days prior to admission. Thus, the 6 patients who died on the first day of admission had actually been ill an average of 11.7 days prior to admission. The author felt that many of the cases reported had been insufficiently studied both clinically and pathologically and that some individuals may have died of "somatic" disease. This is illustrated by the fact that, of 20 patients autopsied, 8 showed diseases at variance with the clinical diagnosis of exhaustion.

Dr. Derby described a similar pattern of signs and symptoms for these patients:

> If a typical case of exhaustion may be analytically demonstrated, we have one entering notably dehydrated, fatigued, but acutely disturbed, with increased pulse rate, and frequently with some degree of temperature elevation. There is frequently a reduced blood pressure and other signs of cardiovascular disturbance rather than pulmonary involvement. The temperature continues elevated and pursues an outstandingly intermittent and septic course and the pulse rate are markedly rapid. If not present previously, the fatigue deepens to exhaustion, and circulatory collapse develops extremely suddenly.[6]

In addition to the symptoms described by Dr. Bell, Dr. Derby observed the following signs on admission:[6]

Dehydration
A rapid pulse
Low blood pressure
Elevated temperature

Temperature elevation could not be substantiated in every case because some patients became too violent to obtain temperatures. Some of the charts, however, indicated a normal temperature for several days prior to death. Vomiting, diarrhea, gastric and rectal hemorrhage indicated a fatal prognosis. Circulatory collapse appeared suddenly following marked exhaustion. The article by Derby is without references. There is no evidence in his article that he was aware of the findings by Dr. Bell in 1849.

In 1934, Dr. G.M. Davidson reported 22 deaths due to "acute lethal excitement" in which there was no anatomical cause for the death either clinically or in the seven cases autopsied.[7] The cases he reviewed were patients admitted to Manhattan State Hospital from 1929 through 1934. The patients were all female aged 21 to 34 years. Their illness was manifested by:

- Sudden onset of illness
- History of delusions and hallucinations
- Acute state lasting from 4 to 20 days
- Extreme psychomotor excitement and restlessness
- Rapid physical decline
- Schizophrenia of the catatonic type in 12 patients
- Postpartum psychoses of catatonic type in 6 patients
- Manic–depressive psychoses of manic and mixed type in 4 patients

These findings are consistent with cases reported by Dr. Bell and Dr. Derby. Again, all the patients are female, perhaps because females with violent behavior were not put in jail during the early part of the century as men were and this accounts for the large numbers of female inpatients in psychiatric care.

In 1934, Kraines published a paper entitled "Bell's Mania (Acute Delirium)," in which he reviewed Bell's paper, and conducted a survey of the literature for additional reports of this entity.[8] He pointed out that there was no uniformity in nomenclature or classification, making it difficult to study this entity. It had been called multiple names: acute delirious mania, delirium grave, typhoma, acute delirium, etc. He stated:

This unusual group presents the syndrome of a sudden onset, with overactivity, great excitement, sleeplessness, apparent delirium, and distorted ideas; without any clear evidence of a definite toxic infectious factor.[8]

In 1938, Dr. N.R. Shulack reported a series of 12 sudden deaths of apparently healthy but "excited" and "active" patients, for which he had no explanation.[9] The group included two patients who had been autopsied. The patients consisted of nine females, aged 23 to 43, and three men, 53 to 66 years of age. Nine had manic–depressive psychosis and three schizophrenia. They had undergone "intensive excitement physically, mentally and emotionally for periods ranging from three days to five months" before dying suddenly and unexpectedly. The majority had elevated temperatures. The causes of death were attributed to "exhaustion from a mental disease."

On reviewing the literature, Shulack found two additional case reports.[10,11] Scheidegger reported 43 deaths in "catatonias" from 1900 to 1928.[10] Of the individuals, 39 were definite or probable schizophrenics, and 4 definite or probable cases of epidemic encephalitis. The ratio of females to males was 7:1. Their symptoms were excitement, fluctuation of temperature, and loss of weight. Autopsies performed on 3 of the individuals produced nonspecific findings. Stefan reported 148 deaths in which death was attributed to "exhaustion"; 139 were female and 9 male.[11] The individuals were described as "overexcited, noisy, screaming, then becoming pale or cyanotic, and 'suddenly they dropped dead.'"[8] The autopsies were said to be non-revealing.

Shulack published a second article in 1944 describing four additional cases of "excited psychotic furors," two of which were fatal, as well as again reviewing the literature.[12] In his review that extended from the early 1900s through 1943, he found 376 cases of sudden death in excited psychotic patients. The four cases he reported involved males between the ages of 23 and 30. This is not unexpected as Shulack was in the military at the time and the four were soldiers. The individuals who survived had the same symptoms as those who died. His four cases presented with the following clinical features:

Sudden onset
Extreme agitation with diffuse anxiety and restlessness
Hallucinations
Assaultive behavior requiring physical restraint

Prior to the onset of cardiac arrest and death, the patients exhibited the following:

A rapid pulse

Low blood pressure

An inconsistent period of hyperpyrexia of hours to days with a slow rise in temperature hours or days prior to death.

In regard to the two patients who died, the first patient was described as being in a constant state of "furor" for 28 hours. He was given barbiturate sedation and placed in restraint. After several days of this behavior and treatment, during which time he was noted to be perspiring profusely, his pulse collapsed and his respirations became rapid, shallow, and irregular. His temperature rose to 109°F and he died suddenly. Diagnosis was unclassified psychosis with an acute state of mania. The second patient to die presented with manic, violent, and assaultive behavior for several days. During this time, he was given a course of treatment consisting of supportive measures of nourishment and sedative medications. Barbiturates, morphine sulfate, and hyoscine hydrobromide were used. The diagnosis was dementia praecox, catatonic type.

In 1947, Adland published a review of "existing material relative to the acute exhaustive syndrome" to demonstrate the "the characteristics of the illness."[13] He itemized the numerous names it was known by, tracing it back to Bell's article in 1849. This article appears to be the most thorough of the reviews published.

Following this last article, "acute exhaustive syndrome," "Bell's mania," or whatever one calls this entity seems to have disappeared from the medical literature. What was notable about these cases was that the victims were young, overwhelming female, had a clinical course of days or weeks, and almost invariably suffered from schizophrenia or bipolar disease.

CURRENT CASES

Beginning in the 1960s, changes in the treatment of patients with endogenous mental disease appear to have led to the disappearance of deaths from the **chronic** form of excited delirium.[4,14–16] Beginning in the 1980s, however, there arose an **acute** form of this entity associated with the use of illegal stimulants, e.g., cocaine. These new deaths are characterized as follows:[1,2,17–21]

- Predominance of male victims
- Preponderance of victims who do not have endogenous mental disease
- Sudden death, minutes or hours after development of excited delirium
- Use of restraints

- Involvement of illegal stimulants or medications that mimic some of the pharmacological properties of the stimulants

Certain psychiatric symptoms originally described by Bell in the chronic form of excited delirium also occur in the acute form of excited delirium syndrome.[3] The importance of these identifying characteristics in assessment criteria for death due to excited delirium syndrome, as well as its prevention, cannot be understated. These symptoms, originally described by Bell, are as follows:

- Sudden onset of symptoms
- Delirium
- Extreme agitation
- Violence with no disposition to yield to overwhelming force
- The need to use physical restraint

The main difference in presentation between the chronic and acute forms of excited delirium syndrome is the time between onset of symptoms and death. In the chronic form, this was a matter of days or weeks. In the acute form, it is minutes or hours.

Deaths of mental patients from the "acute" form of excited delirium syndrome probably always occurred. The large number of chronic deaths masked them, however. The sudden "appearance" of these acute deaths in mental health facilities has led to hasty, inflammatory, and unsupported accusations of wrongful death by families of the deceased, attorneys, and the press. Unsubstantiated accusations of abuse and misuse of physical and chemical restraint interventions in dealing with violent patients have been made against medical personnel.

The *Hartford Courant* brought the problem of death due to excited delirium in relationship to mental disease to public attention with a series of articles entitled "Deadly Restraint" published in 1998.[22] It outlined 142 deaths occurring over a period of 10 years nationwide in mental health facilities. Approximately 27% of the deaths involved females. There is insufficient information provided in this article regarding to how many of the cases actually involve excited delirium. The only common factor in most of the deaths was the use of restraint. Some deaths were obviously not due to excited delirium. Thus, there are deaths due to blunt trauma, an overdose of drugs, smoke inhalation, congenital heart disease, sepsis, etc.

What is most annoying about this article is that, while it does communicate a serious medical problem involving mental patients, instead of approaching it in an unbiased, scientific way and attempting to find out what is occurring, the writers reduce the problem to a two-dimensional, black-and-white, cartoon. The report presents an inflammatory and incorrect description of treatment by medical staff in response to violent patients. In the article, the authors display a lack of knowledge about medicine and medical procedures coupled with a naïveté that is astounding for journalists. They place greater weight in statements by mentally ill individuals and guilt-ridden relatives than those by medical personnel. The former are always telling the truth; the latter are uncaring, brutal liars. They indulge in inflammatory verbiage intended to turn off the mind and appeal to passion. Thus, the patient is "slammed face-down on the floor, … arms were yanked across her chest, her wrists gripped from behind by a mental health aide."[22] "Her limp body was rolled into a blanket and dumped in an 8 × 10 foot room used to seclude dangerous patients."[22]

PSYCHOPHARMACOLOGY AND THE DISAPPEARANCE OF THE CHRONIC FORM OF EXCITED DELIRIUM

Beginning in the 1960s, changes in the treatment of patients with endogenous mental disease, coupled with the closure of long-term care mental institutions, led to the era of "psychopharmacology."[14–16,23] The introduction of antipsychotic drugs allowed patients with schizophrenia and other serious mental disorders, who had previously been confined to mental psychiatric facilities, to be released into the community. Many of these individuals then stopped taking their medications and relapsed into their psychoses. These patients would then be encountered by law enforcement personnel called to respond to reports of bizarre behavior and violence.

It is the belief of the authors that the disappearance of the "chronic" form of excited delirium syndrome in the psychiatric patient was due to the introduction of effective antipsychotic medication for treatment of psychotic patients. The first of these medications was chlorpromazine, a phenothiazine. Chlorpromazine not only targeted specific psychotic symptoms, but it also possessed sedative qualities. A surgeon, Dr. Laborit, accidentally discovered the usefulness of chlorpromazine in the treatment of patients suffering from schizophrenia.[24] While experimenting with a form of anesthesia, which he called "hibernation," Dr. Laborit noticed that one of the drugs he was using, "chlorpromazine," produced strange effects he likened to a "chemical lobotomy" and recommended its use in psychiatry.

It was released for clinical use in May 2, 1951, and given for the first time to psychiatric patients on January 19, 1952, at Val de Grace, a military hospital in Paris. It would not be until the 1960s, however, that chlorpromazine would be sanctioned by the U.S. Veterans Administration as an effective treatment for psychotic patients.[15]

Prior to the introduction of chlorpromazine, therapeutic treatment of the mentally ill by means of paraldehyde, chloral hydrate, amobarbital, and phenobarbital did little to prevent recurrent psychotic symptoms.[14] This was because the primary effect of these drugs was sedative. They did not act on the underling psychotic condition.

> In public institutions, the great error of the pre-neuroleptic era was that sedation was often considered an excellent outcome. In the neuroleptic era, the measure of an excellent outcome became the control of positive symptoms, in particular agitation.[14]

Chlorpromazine not only possessed sedative qualities but it also targeted specific psychotic symptoms. The introduction of antipsychotic medications combining the therapeutic effects of inducing strong sedation to interrupt and reduce the cycle of physical and mental deterioration as well as reducing and controlling psychotic symptoms was a revolutionary event in the treatment of psychotic patients.

> It is difficult to communicate to younger colleagues the miracle that 150 to 300 mg of chlorpromazine a day appeared to be to the house officers of 1956. It not only sedated the patients but actually made them less psychotic.[14]

The use of antipsychotic medication was the pivotal reason that deaths from chronic excited delirium syndrome disappeared from institutions and the medical literature.[4] Chlorpromazine and other drugs that followed it provided a therapeutic means to treat the violent and unmanageable psychotic patient. The escalating cycles of extreme physical deterioration and mental decline that resulted in the chronic form of excited delirium death witnessed by Dr. Bell and others disappeared. The cycle of agitation, delirium, violence, and the need for physical restraint often encountered by mental health caregivers could be arrested.[14,15]

Although chlorpromazine is still considered an effective antipsychotic medication by some, it is not without serious side effects, e.g., neuroleptic malignant syndrome, extrapyramidal reactions, tardive dyskinesia, and severe liver and cardiovascular disease.[16,23] As drug companies attempted to manufacture newer antipsychotic drugs with reduced side effects, the strong sedative qualities present in chlorpromazine were eliminated so that the patients on these drugs could more readily be released into society. Elimination of this characteristic may possibly make an individual more susceptible to development of acute excited delirium syndrome.

ACUTE EXCITED DELIRIUM

The new era of psychopharmacology in the treatment of mentally ill patients saw the disappearance of the "chronic" form of excited delirium syndrome. What we now encounter in mental health institutions, hospitals, and in the public arena are deaths from the "acute" form of the excited delirium syndrome. Individuals with a psychiatric history dying of the acute form of excited delirium syndrome virtually always have a history of schizophrenia or bipolar disease. Occasionally deaths are associated with mental retardation.[25] In many cases, the medications the patient is taking may inadvertently predispose the patient to sudden death.

Chronically ill mental patients once treated in long-term care facilities are now placed on antipsychotic medications and released into the community to be treated on an outpatient basis. The problem with this concept of therapy is that after release the patients may stop taking their medication and relapse into their psychoses. Once released, there is no way to force them to take their medications. In addition, there is a lack of outpatient facilities to help these individuals if they seek help. The discontinuation of medications and lack of follow-up care needed by the mentally ill patient in the community setting result in situational family and community violence. The pattern of hallucinations, aggression, and violent behavior in individuals with schizophrenia and other serious mental disturbances reappears. Law enforcement personnel are now called to respond to these individuals' violent behavior. As they are not medical personnel, they have to resort to chemical and physical restraints earlier in their intervention in these cases. Complicating the picture for law enforcement personnel is that most people in the community presenting with the symptoms of excited delirium currently are not individuals with intrinsic mental disease but individuals whose symptoms are due to illicit stimulants. The officers cannot differentiate between them. In fact, such differentiation is not possible by medical personnel without a history and/or toxicology testing. Because of this, the initial response to both groups of individuals is the same.

Some individuals in excited delirium are brought into emergency rooms, usually by law enforcement. On initial presentation, one cannot determine if the excited delirium is due to intrinsic mental disease or to drugs. In the emergency room, one has the theoretical advantage that one has access to medications. Since such individuals are virtually always struggling, medication has to be given intramuscularly. In many cases, it seems to have no effect. In cases where the individual dies, toxicology often fails to reveal the presence of this medication in the blood, indicating that death has occurred before there was time to absorb the drug into the blood. Thus, there was no therapeutic effect from administration of this drug.

Death occurring from "excited delirium syndrome, whether due to intrinsic mental disease or use of stimulants, is characterized by:[3]

- Acute onset of symptoms (minutes to hours)
- Delirium with acute, transient disturbance in consciousness and cognition; disorientation; disorganized and inconsistent thought processes; inability to distinguish reality from hallucinations; disturbances in speech; disorientation to time and place; misidentification of individuals
- Combative and/or violent behavior
- Use of physical restraint
- Sudden cardiac death within minutes to hours after development of symptoms
- Lack of response to cardiopulmonary resuscitation (CPR)
- A history of either stimulant abuse or endogenous mental disease

By 1980, the concept of death due to excited delirium (Bell's mania) was for the most part unknown to most members of the medical profession. The only branch of medicine still familiar with this entity was the psychiatric community.[4] Even here, however, this knowledge was beginning to fade, as deaths from the traditional presentation of excited delirium, Bell's mania, disappeared. The occasional acute death in association with excited delirium went unnoticed or was ascribed to an unusual reaction to the use of an antipsychotic medication or to "heart disease." All this was soon to change with the widespread use of cocaine and methamphetamine.

In 1981, Fishbain and Wetli published an article in the *Annals of Emergency Medicine* reintroducing the general medical community to the concept of death in association with excited delirium.[1] Unlike cases published prior to this time, which involved psychiatric patients, the individual in this paper was suffering from excited delirium due to acute cocaine intoxication resulting from "body packing." A cocaine "body packer" is an individual who smuggles cocaine either by swallowing packets of the drug in plastic bags, balloons, or condoms or by inserting such packets into the rectum. If one of these packets leaks or breaks, it can cause death by acute cocaine intoxication. The usual symptoms are tachycardia, hypertension, hyperthermia, stupor, and seizures. In the case reported, the patient had been able to remove all but one packet from his body. When he began to develop cocaine toxicity, he went to the hospital claiming that he had ingested 20 tablets of propoxyphene. Following admission, he became progressively more agitated, confused, disoriented, and incoherent. He ran through the halls screaming and threatening staff. The staff then decided to restrain him, which required six men to accomplish. He was then given chlorpromazine, sodium amytal, and haloperidol. At 3½ hours after his last dose, he was found in respiratory arrest and could not be resuscitated. The diagnosis of cocaine intoxication was missed because, instead of presenting with the traditional symptoms of cocaine toxicity, he presented with confusion, disorientation, agitation, aggressive and violent behavior, i.e., psychiatric symptomatology of excited delirium. Autopsy findings were essentially negative. This case is atypical for excited delirium syndrome in that death occurred a few hours after institution of restraint. The importance of this paper is that it reintroduced the concept of linkage between sudden death and excited delirium, although in the context of cocaine intoxication.

The aforementioned case originated on the East Coast of the U.S., specifically Miami. At the same time, on the West Coast, an apparently different entity was being reported which would soon be associated with deaths due to excited delirium. In 1982, Reay and Eisele reported two deaths allegedly resulting from the use of neck holds by law enforcement personnel.[26] The first case involved a 58-year-old man with a history of heart disease and a prior episode of cardiac arrest from which he was resuscitated. Following this episode, he began to have psychiatric problems. His wife sought involuntary commitment for him. When two officers came to take him to the hospital, a brief but violent struggle ensued. One officer attempted a carotid hold and both he and the victim fell to the ground. At this time, the victim became lifeless. Witnesses including the family stated that the hold was in place only seconds. The autopsy revealed a fracture of the left cornu of the thyroid cartilage and petechiae in the conjunctivae. The heart was enlarged and showed interstitial fibrosis. Death was ascribed to cardiac disease, with "neck compression" a contributory factor. The manner of death was described as homicide. The fracture of the thyroid cartilage was attributed to the hold. What had started out as a carotid sleeper hold became a bar or choke hold. The fracture was, of course, just a marker of pressure applied and had nothing to do with the death. The petechiae could have been due to the neck pressure or just acute cardiac failure. Petechiae are seen in a number of conditions including fatal heart attacks. The authors of the current text feel that making the neck hold a contributory factor in this death is not justified. It was the struggle itself that caused the heart attack, not an event that lasted only several seconds. We would not classify this case as a death due to excited delirium syndrome, but rather attribute the cause of death to the heart disease.

The second case involved a 35-year-old man with manic–depressive psychosis.[26] While in jail for threatening his wife, he became combative and disruptive. He was handcuffed and moved to a solitary cell. Here, he continued his disruptive behavior. At this time, he was forced facedown on the bunk and his handcuffs were removed and replaced by flex cuffs. As this was occurring, a guard had put a "carotid sleeper" hold on him. The patient ceased struggling and the guards left the cell. A few minutes later, he was found apneic. CPR was unsuccessful. At autopsy, there were petechiae of the conjunctivae and a fracture of the left superior horn of the thyroid cartilage. As in the last case, a carotid sleeper hold had become a choke hold. Inadvertent conversion of a carotid sleeper hold to a choke hold is not unexpected in situations where two individuals are engaged in a struggle. In this case, the cause of death was said to be the neck hold. Deaths due to neck holds are actually cases of manual strangulation. One would have to maintain the hold 2 to 3 minutes to cause cessation of respiration. There is no indication or allegation that the neck hold was maintained that long.

In this paper, there was a discussion of the phenomenon of carotid sinus hypersensitivity. This is said to play a part in producing death in individuals who have had a neck hold applied. This theory does not bear up to close scrutiny, as discussed in detail in Chapter 3, where it is shown that in virtually all cases involving use of neck holds they play no role in causing death.

Back on the East Coast, the increasing use of cocaine resulted in a flood of deaths due to what we now call excited delirium syndrome. In 1985, Wetli and Fishbain, who 3 years before had described the death of a body packer, now reported seven deaths in association with excited delirium in a paper entitled "Cocaine-Induced Psychosis and Sudden Death in Recreational Cocaine Users."[2] Of the seven cases reported, all presented in excited delirium and all were restrained. Five died in police custody and two in medical custody. Of the latter two cases, one experienced respiratory arrest 2 hours after admission, was resuscitated but died 6 hours after admission. The second experienced a respiratory arrest 4 hours after admission, with resuscitation and death on the fourth hospital day. A laparotomy conducted immediately after the arrest revealed two iatrogenic perforations of the bowel.

In none of the seven cases were neck holds used and none was placed in situations where mechanical asphyxia was possible. Of the five dying in police custody, three were hog-tied and two were only handcuffed. The authors made no mention of restraints contributing or causing death. One would have to conclude that they placed no significance on use of restraints.

Back on the West Coast, in 1988, Reay et al.[27] conducted a series of experiments to determine the effects on peripheral oxygen saturation and heart rate that occur when an individual is hog-tied and placed prone following exercise. Peripheral oxygen saturation and heart rate were determined using a pulse oximeter. They concluded that hog-tie restraint prolongs recovery from exercise as determined by changes in peripheral oxygen saturation and heart rate. They speculated that restriction of thoracic respiratory movements could be one of the mechanisms for this occurrence and recommended that positional restraint and its effects should be considered in the investigation of individuals restrained in the prone position. In the last sentence of this paper they stated, "Additional research is needed to better understand the pathophysiology involved in these deaths." Unfortunately, additional work was not done until 1997.[28] Their 1988 paper, however, led to misconceptions regarding the physiological results of the use of restraints and numerous lawsuits.

In 1992, Reay et al.[29] published a paper entitled "Positional Asphyxia during Law Enforcement Transport." They described three cases in which individuals died after being hog-tied and placed prone in the rear of police vehicles. One individual died while being transported to a hospital and the other two while they were being transported to jail.. All had exhibited symptoms of excited delirium prior to restraint. Two of the three had a history of endogenous mental disease and one was under the influence of alcohol, marijuana, and LSD.

In the first case, the individual, a manic–depressive, was hog-tied and placed prone on the rear seat of a patrol car. He arrested during a 5 to 7 minute trip to the hospital. At autopsy, he was 73 inches tall, weighed 267 lb and was described as having an "abundant abdominal panniculus." In the second case, the individual was hog-tied and placed prone on a narrow, plastic one-piece seat. During transport, he slipped off the seat and became wedged between the front- and backseats. The third individual, who had a history of schizophrenia, was hog-tied and placed prone on the floor of the rear of a police car, such that his head, shoulders, and chest were in the foot well behind the driver's seat, his right flank over the drive shaft, and his legs in a flexed position on the rear bench seat behind the front passenger seat. All three deaths were ascribed to positional asphyxia. The authors of this text agree with the cause of death in the last two cases, but have doubts about the first case. Reay et al. felt that obesity with the large abdominal panniculus interfered with respiration in this case. In the other two cases, mechanical displacement of the abdomen resulted in asphyxia and death.[29]

Reay et al.[29] stated in their paper that positional asphyxia occurs when the position of the body interferes with respiration and that one generally needs one or more contributory factors to explain the inability of victims to remove themselves from the hostile environment, e.g., restraint, entrapment, alcohol or drugs, physical disability.

A report issued in 1992 illustrates the thinking at the time that use of restraints and carotid holds were acceptable with certain restrictions. In 1992, the San Diego Police Department issued a report prepared by a Death in Custody Task Force, which was widely circulated among police agencies nationwide.[30] The task force investigated seven deaths in custody. Two of the deaths occurred following use of a choke hold; the other five following use of restraints. Two of the five involved hog-tying. Based on its investigation the task force made a series of recommendations. It did not ban either the carotid hold or hog-tying but rather set restrictions on their use. In regard to hog-tying, the police department banned "the practice of transporting subjects in a 'hogtied' and prone position in the back of a police vehicle." The recommendations of this report placed greater stress on the dangers of carotid holds than restraint.

Up to this time, the concept that the mechanism of death in excited delirium is due almost exclusively to restraint had not been solidified. It was not until 1993, in an article by O'Halloran and Lewman,[31] that the association of restraint and asphyxiation, hog-tying and death were codified in the concept of "restraint asphyxia" or "positional asphyxia." These authors reported 11 cases of individuals in excited delirium who died following restraint in a prone position: 9 were hog-tied, 1 tied to a hospital gurney, and 1 held prone manually. Of the individuals, 6 were under the influence of cocaine, 1 methamphetamine, 1 LSD, and 3 had intrinsic mental disease. Two of the hog-tied individuals died in the back of police vehicles. All individuals presented with excited delirium with the symptoms less than 1 to 6 hours in duration. All required several individuals to control and restrain them; all were restrained prone; all continued to struggle when initially restrained.

The authors of the paper said its purpose was to alert interested parties that "the hog-tied prone position in delirious people can have sudden, unexpected, lethal consequences, and requires close monitoring or alternative restraint methods to prevent sudden death." The authors felt that the mechanism of death in these cases was a sudden cardiac arrhythmia or respiratory arrest due to the combination of at least three possible factors "relating to increased oxygen demands and decreased oxygen delivery":

1. Stress on the heart due to catecholamine release from the excited delirium
2. The hyperactivity of excited delirium; the resultant struggle with police and/or medical personnel and struggling against the restraints increased oxygen demand
3. Hog-tying impaired breathing by inhibiting chest wall and diaphragmatic movement in face of the increased oxygen demands

This paper obviously based its opinion as to impairment of respiration on the work of Reay et al.[29] The problem was that Reay et al.'s findings were wrong. This would not be known, however, until 1997.[28]

The year 1995 saw the publication of a paper by Stratton et al., which described what they thought was the first report of sudden death associated with excited delirium and restraint during transport by medical personnel.[32] This paper is important because the two individuals in this study were being monitored when they died and resuscitation was begun immediately. Both individuals were hog-tied. The first individual was a 35-year-old male on methamphetamine who was transported hog-tied and prone. His heart rate went from 136 to 60 beats/minute, went up to 102, and then to asystole, all within a minute. The other individual on cocaine and methamphetamine suffered a rapid asystolic arrest. Despite the fact that the arrests were observed and despite immediate institution of resuscitation by trained and equipped Advanced Life Support (ALS) personnel, both patients died.

In 1997, Ruttenber et al.[18] reported 58 deaths due to cocaine-induced excited delirium that occurred in Dade County, Florida from 1979 to 1990. These cases were discussed and elaborated on in a subsequent article published in 1999.[19] In the report, 93.1% of the individuals were male. The average age was 31.3 years, and 97.4% (38 cases) of the individuals for whom body temperature was obtained were hyperthermic. Because body temperature was taken only when it was felt to be elevated, this number is somewhat distorted in terms of frequency of hyperthermia. In the 1999 paper, Ruttenber et al. proposed that rhabdomyolysis and excited delirium due to cocaine are different stages of the same syndrome and that changes in the dopamine receptors and transporters in the brain cause the syndrome.[19] These changes were said to be due to "chronic and intense use of cocaine rather than the acute effects of the drug." Chronic cocaine use decreases the density of D1 receptors in the brain but not the D2 receptors. In individuals with excited delirium, the number of D2 receptors in the thermoregulatory centers of the hypothalamus is reduced. This can lead to hyperthermia as D2 receptors decrease body core temperature. The authors felt that hyperthermia and hyperactivity both together and individually play roles in the development of rhabdomyolysis.

The concept that most deaths due to excited delirium syndrome are due to positional or restraint asphyxia was dealt what many consider a death blow in 1997 by the work of Chan et al.[28] Unfortunately, some individuals wedded to the positional asphyxia theory act as if Chan's paper does not exist. The theory of death due to positional asphyxia rested on the work of Reay et al. in 1988.[27] They claimed that restraint applied after exercise resulted in a prolongation of the heart rate and oxygen saturation recovery time. There are several problems with Reay et al.'s paper:

1. There was no assessment of actual ventilatory and respiratory mechanisms in individuals in the restraint position.

2. The authors reported a drop in oxygen saturation with exercise even though most physiologic work shows improvement in arterial oxygenation with mild to moderate exercise.
3. The preferred method of assessing arterial blood oxygenation is arterial blood gas measurement. Measurement by pulse-oximetry is potentially inaccurate particularly during exercise.

Reay et al. did suggest that additional work should be performed on this topic.

Chan et al.[28] decided to repeat the experiments using a more systematic approach and more sophisticated technology. Pulmonary function testing (forced vital capacity; forced expiratory volume in 1 second and maximal voluntary ventilation) was performed on 15 individuals, ages 18 to 40 years, in the sitting, supine, prone, and restraint position (hog-tying). The subjects were then subjected to two exercise periods and two rest periods. Exercise consisted of 4 minutes on an exercise bicycle. During the rest periods, determinations of arterial blood gas; pulse rate; oxygen saturation by CO-oximetry and pulse oximetry and pulmonary function testing (PFT) were performed. Determinations at the rest periods were made with the subject alternatively in the sitting position and restraint position. Changes in the heart rate occurred with exercise with a maximum of 164 ± 18.9 beats/minute at the beginning of the sitting rest period and 174 ± 15.3 beats/minute at the beginning of the restraint rest period.

Placing individuals in the restraint position after exercise resulted in restrictive pulmonary functioning as measured by PFT. However, the PFT changes while statistically significant **were not clinically relevant**. Based on arterial PO_2 and CO-oximetry, oxygenation of blood increased with exercise, what one would expect and in contrast to Reay et al.'s findings.[27] Most importantly, there was no evidence of hypoxia in the restraint position after exercise with no evidence of hypercapnia either during exercise or in restraint.

Chan et al. concluded:[40]

1. There is no evidence that body position while in the "hog-tie" or "hobble" restraint position as a factor in and of itself causes hypoventilation or asphyxiation.
2. Factors other than body positioning are more important determinants for the sudden, unexpected deaths that occur in individuals who are placed in the restraint position.

The authors acknowledged that individuals who are extremely obese, with a large abdominal girth and a body mass index (BMI) greater than 30 kg/m² may be at a greater risk for developing restrictive pulmonary function secondary to abdominal compression from body positioning.

The same month that Chan et al.'s article was published, an editorial appeared in the *British Medical Journal* entitled, "Acute Excited States and Sudden Death: Much Journalism, Little Evidence."[33] The authors, Farnham and Kennedy, made a number of points.

1. Excited delirium is commonly associated with cocaine and other stimulants, less commonly with schizophrenia.
2. Before neuroleptics were introduced, death in these cases was alluded to as "exhaustion."
3. Acute excited states are a medical emergency with a serious mortality.
4. Death is preceded by a cycle of alternating struggle and collapse.
5. There is a lack of anatomical findings to explain death.
6. If a state of excited delirium cannot be prevented or the situation defused, and the individual is a danger to themselves or others, the only other options are restraint, seclusion, or medication or a combination of them.

Even though this article was written before the article by Chan et al. was published, the authors stated in regard to the concept that death was due to positional asphyxia: "this suggestion must be treated with caution."[40] Farnham and Kennedy pointed to the source of the problem with deaths due to excited delirium, as perceived by the legal system, the public, and the press: "Legal reasoning favours single proximate causes rather than medical conditions, but the intervention most proximate to the time of death is not necessarily the cause of death. Similarly, popular journalism favors controversy and blame rather than balance and exploration."[33]

In 1998, Pollanen et al.[34] reported 21 sudden unexpected deaths in association with excited delirium. All exhibited symptoms of excited delirium: bizarre or hyperactive behavior, paranoia, shouting, thrashing about, and ranting. The most interesting aspect of this report is the distribution of cases by etiology of the excited delirium. In 12 individuals (57%), the excited delirium was due to psychiatric disorder; in 8 (38%) to cocaine, and in 1 a combination of alcohol, morphine, diazepam, acetaminophen, and marijuana. The mean age was 33 years, 20 were males, all were restrained, and 18 prone. The report stated 3 had pressure on the neck and 8 of the 18 restrained prone also had chest compression. All suddenly lapsed into "tranquility" shortly after being restrained, and 19 died at the time of restraint. The other 2 were resuscitated but in a deep coma and died several days later. The authors felt that they "could not establish a definitive causal link between unexpected death and restraint in people with excited delirium." Their conclusion was "restraint may contribute to the death of people in states of excited delirium, and further studies to test this hypothesis are recommended." The authors did not appear to be aware of the work of Chan et al.,[28] which may have been due to the close proximity in the publication of the two papers.

The paper by Stratton et al.[35] in 2001 is interesting and highly relevant in that all the reported 18 deaths due to excited delirium syndrome were witnessed by Emergency Medical Sevices (EMS) personnel who were able to institute immediate CPR. The study involved 216 cases of excited delirium witnessed by EMS personnel. In all cases, the individuals had their wrists and ankles bound and attached behind their backs; i.e., they were hog-tied. Of the 216, 20 experienced cardiopulmonary arrest and died. Two deaths were excluded from the study, one because of pulmonary emboli and the other because of ligature marks and contusions of the neck. The presenting pattern for the 18 deaths was similar:

Excited delirium
Hobble restraint (hog-tied)
Cessation of the struggle with labored or agonal breathing and then cardiopulmonary death

Review of the data indicates that 9 individuals had heart weights greater than 400 g. The authors of this text consider all male hearts above 400 g to be enlarged. Of these 9 cases, 3 had a weight greater than 400 g but less than 450 g and 6 a weight of greater than 450 g. Of the 9 cases in which the heart was not enlarged, 1 showed myocardial fibrosis and another right ventricular hypertrophy. Thus in our opinion, only 7 of the 18 cases had normal hearts.

Cocaine and or methamphetamine was present in 78% of the cases: 7 showed cocaine, 4 methamphetamine, and 3 cocaine and methamphetamine. In only 1 case did the individual have neither cardiac disease nor the presence of cocaine and/or methamphetamine.

All cardiopulmonary arrests were preceded by a short period (estimated at 5 minutes or less) during which the struggle had ceased and the individual had labored or shallow breathing. Of the 18 witnessed cases of arrest, none was able to be resuscitated even with immediate intervention by EMS personnel.

In the study, the BMI was determined for each individual, and conclusions were drawn from these determinations. Because the authors of this study are clinicians, they are likely unaware of the problem with utilizing postmortem height and weight determinations. While measurement of weight is generally reliable, even here there are some problems in that there are no standards regarding how a body should be weighed. Thus, individuals are weighed dressed, undressed, in body transport bags, and with resuscitative gear on the body or cart. Measurement of height is often off by 1 to 2 inches, if not more, depending on the care with which it is taken. Height and weight measurements taken from records in which the patient/deceased provided this information is suspect in that individuals often style themselves lighter and taller.

Based on the BMI, Stratton et al.[32] note that 50% of the victims were obese. This seems significant until one realizes that 64.5% of the adult population in the United States is either overweight or obese.[36] In addition, obesity is higher in the lower socioeconomic group, which tends to represent the vast bulk of deaths due to excited delirium syndrome.

By 2000, despite the work of Chan et al., the proposed mechanism of death in excited delirium syndrome was for many individuals still positional asphyxia and/or neck holds.[28] Hog-tying was seen as the main culprit in causing death and its use was banned by many police departments. It was also recommended that individuals after being restrained be placed on their sides. That deaths such as this occurred in mental health facilities was not even discussed. Unfortunately, even with the elimination of hog-tying and the placing of individuals on their sides rather than prone, the number of deaths due to excited delirium syndrome stayed steady, if not increased. The medical profession often ignored the work of Chan et al., although this work had put a major crimp in lawsuits against police departments where claims of positional asphyxia were made.[28] That the legal profession accepted the work of Chan et al. while the medical profession still espoused theories that had been proved wrong by scientific testing is fascinating. While some individuals acted as if Chan et al.'s work had never been performed, others challenged it on illogical grounds. Some stated that the work was not relevant in that Chan's group used only healthy individuals in their testing. Of course, the individuals dying from excited delirium are not usually cardiac cripples. If an individual in fact died during restraint with severe active disease, e.g., a pulmonary embolus or a large acute myocardial infarct, most medical practitioners would assign the cause of death to these conditions rather than positional asphyxia. In fact, as one reviews the cases being reported, one is struck that the individuals involved tend to be young and relatively healthy. The only consistent finding is enlargement of the heart in individuals whose excited delirium is due to cocaine and methamphetamine abuse. This is consistent with the observations that chronic abusers of cocaine and methamphetamine tend to show enlargement of the heart.[21]

In an attempt to counter Chan et al.'s work, some individuals now claim that the death is due to compromise in ventilation occurring when an officer/medical worker applies bodyweight to the upper torso of an individual in an attempt to restrain the individual and/or prevent further struggle. This is usually accomplished by lying across an individual's back, or by applying pressure on the back with a knee or hands. This contention/theory is discussed in Chapter 3 in more detail. It must be realized that this is a hypothesis and the only attempt to confirm it experimentally seems to have disproved it.

The first significant mention of this concept was by O'Halloran and Frank in a paper published in 2000.[25] They also stated that they felt that the term "restraint asphyxia" should be used in such cases rather than positional asphyxia. What is most fascinating about the paper is that there is absolutely no mention of the work by Chan et al.[28] One wonders how one could in 2000 discuss the etiology of excited delirium syndrome without mentioning the papers of Chan et al.

O'Halloran and Frank report 21 cases of "asphyxial death" during prone restraint.[25] All 21 individuals were male with ages ranging between 17 and 45; 8 had a history of chronic mental illness. All were in a prone position. There was no use of choke holds. The uselessness of the hog-tie ban is illustrated by the fact that only 4 of these individuals were hog-tied. Of these, 3 had enlarged hearts (>400 g), 1 exhibited myocardial fibrosis. Toxicology revealed that 1 had a very high blood level of cocaine; another methamphetamine and cocaine metabolite, and another methamphetamine. The fourth had a 3-year history of psychosis and a therapeutic level of haloperidol in the blood. This was one of the individuals with an enlarged heart.

Of the 17 individuals who were not hog-tied:

1. Two were severely mentally retarded. One had therapeutic levels of doxepin and thioridazine. The other had a minimally enlarged heart with microscopic foci of fibrosis and therapeutic blood levels of thioridazine, mesoridazine, and fluoxetine.
2. Three had markedly enlarged hearts (500, 750, and 510 g). The individual with the 500 g heart had a blood cocaine level of 1.2 mg/l, benzoylecgonine of 6.4, and cocaethylene of 0.4 mg/l.
3. One individual with a history of chronic alcohol and cocaine abuse had an enlarged heart (480 g) and cirrhosis of the liver.
4. One individual had a 450 g heart and subendocardial fibrosis.
5. Three had enlarged hearts (430, 430, and 450 g) with cocaine present. Cocaine levels were 5.4, 0.23, and 1.2 mg/l, respectively.
6. One had left anterior coronary artery bridging and cocaine.
7. One individual with bipolar disease had an enlarged heart (430 g).
8. Two had cocaine present (1.1 mg/l, 0.02).
9. One had a methamphetamine level of 1.7 mg/l with a mildly enlarged heart (410 g).
10. Two were chronic schizophrenics, one of whom had chlorpromazine and diphenhydramine in therapeutic levels.

The most striking fact about these cases is the fact that 15 had heart disease of some sort. In addition, 11 had stimulants (8 cocaine, 2 methamphetamine, and 1 cocaine and methamphetamine) in their blood. There were 8 individuals with a history of chronic mental illness, excluding drug abuse, and 3 had heart disease. Of the remaining 5, 4 were on medications that are associated with induced prolongation of the QT interval and sudden death, e.g., thioridazine. Thus, after reviewing the paper one realizes that virtually all of the individuals who died had conditions that combined with hyperactivity of the sympathetic nervous system are more than enough to explain the death without invoking asphyxia as a mechanism. The authors are making the classic mistake of confusing proximity of an action, e.g., restraint, with causality, an error in logic identified by Aristotle more than 2000 years ago.[21]

In 2001, Park et al.[37] reported two deaths due to excited delirium occurring under the supervision of medical personnel when they became unresponsive. The paper gives a brief review of the presentation of such cases. They point out that such cases are associated with schizophrenia, bipolar disease, intoxication with cocaine, and alcohol withdrawal. In the first case, the individual had a history of schizophrenia. The individual was manually restrained after a struggle and strapped to a gurney in a supine position. He entered the ambulance alert, became less responsive, and developed cardiopulmonary arrest with asystole within 15 minutes. CPR was instituted. He arrived at the emergency room is asystole and was pronounced dead 22 minutes after arrival. The second individual was a woman with a history of substance abuse brought to the emergency room with symptoms of excited delirium. Minutes after arrival she was administered haloperidol intramuscularly and hospital police had to restrain her. She was in a sitting position on a gurney with her wrists handcuffed to her ankles when she experienced cardiopulmonary arrest. An electrocardiogram (EKG) showed pulseless electrical activity. Cardiac activity was restored following CPR. Her rectal temperature was 105°F. Urine toxicology was positive for cocaine and opiates. She died 9 days later of anoxic encephalopathy complicated by rhabdomyolysis.

The authors of the paper concluded that the death of the first individual was consistent with catecholamine-induced sudden death due to lack of restraint in a prone position. In the second case, the authors felt that her position and the rhabdomyolysis may have played some role in the death. Following publication of this article, Vilke and Chan wrote a letter to the editor in regard to it.[38] They stated their position that there is no medical literature supporting the theory that death from asphyxiation in a restrained or prone position is a common occurrence. They also pointed out that additional work by these two authors in regard to individuals in sitting, prone, and supine positions demonstrated that body position does not have any physiologically significant impact on pulmonary function. In a response by the authors, they added that they felt that positioning may have played a part in the death of their second case in that she was morbidly obese.[39]

As mentioned previously, some individuals now claim that the death is due to compromise in ventilation occurring when a police officer/medical worker applies bodyweight to the upper torso of an individual in an attempt to restrain the individual and prevent further struggle. This is usually accomplished by lying across an individual's back or by applying pressure on the back with a knee or hands. Of course, as usual, no scientific backing is given for this theory. Chan et al.[40] address this theory in a paper published in 2004. They conducted a series of experiments in which weights were applied to individuals restrained in the hog-tie or hobble position. This position is rarely used nowadays and is the most extreme of the restraint positions that have been used. Most deaths in restrained individuals now being reported involve two modalities: either the individual is held down in a four-point restraint or the individual's hands are cuffed behind the back and the ankles tied together. Thus, Chan et al.'s scenario utilizes the most extreme form of restraint. The authors utilized three positions: sitting; hog-tie with 25 lb on the back, and hog-tie with 50 lb on the back. They then measured pulse oximetry, end-tidal CO_2 levels, forced vital capacity (FVC), and forced expiratory volume in 1 second (FEV1). FVC and FEV1, while significantly lower in the restraint positions compared to the sitting, were not significantly different with or without weight force. More importantly, the mean oxygen saturation levels were above 95% and mean end-tidal CO_2 levels below 45 mm Hg for all positions. Thus, the hog-tie position, with or without 25 and 50 lb of weight force, while producing a restrictive pulmonary function pattern, did not produce any evidence of hypoxia or hypoventilation (no evidence of hypoxia, oxygen desaturation, hypercapnia, or CO_2 retention). Some would argue if one puts more weight on the individual eventually hypoxia will result. This is of course true. If one parks a car on an individual's chest, the individual will asphyxiate. There is, however, no proof that the amount of force placed on individuals by kneeling on them or lying across their bodies compromises respiration. In fact, these activities are performed daily by police making arrests of violent individuals and medical personnel restraining violent individuals. The fact is that many of the investigators promulgating the theories of restraint asphyxia have never had contact with or attempted to restrain a violent individual.

REFERENCES

1. Fishbain, D.A. and Wetli, C.V. Cocaine intoxication, delirium and death in a body packer. *Ann Emerg Med.* 10:531–532, 1981.
2. Wetli, C.V. and Fishbain, D.A. Cocaine-induced psychosis and sudden death in recreational cocaine users. *J Forensic Sci.* 30(3)873–880, 1985.
3. Bell, L.V. On a form of disease resembling some advanced stages of mania and fever. *Am. J. Insanity* 6:97–127, 1849.
4. Wendkos, M.H. Acute exhaustive mania. In *Sudden Death and Psychiatric Illness.* Medical & Scientific Books, New York, 1979, chap. 10.
5. Kraepelin, E. *Dementia Praecox and Paraphrenia,* fascimile 1919, Engl. transl. Translated by Barclay, R.M. and Robertson, G.M. Robert E. Krieger, Huntington, New York, 1971.
6. Derby, I. Manic–depressive "exhaustion" deaths. *Psychiatr. Q.* 7:436–449, 1933.
7. Davidson, G.M. Concerning the cause of death in certain psychoses. *Am. J. Psychiatr.* 91:41–49, 1934.
8. Kraines, S.H. Bell's mania (acute delirium). *Am. J. Psychiatr.* 91:29–40, 1934.
9. Shulack, N.R. Sudden "exhaustive" death in excited patients. *Psychiatr. Q.* 12:282–293, 1938.
10. Scheidegger, W. Katatone-Todesfaelle. *Psych. Klin. Burghoelzli,* v 1900–1928, J. Springer, Zurich, 1929. Cited by Davidson, G.M. Concerning the cause of death in certain psychoses. *Am. J. Psychiatr.* 91:41–49, 1934; and Shulack, N.R. Sudden "exhaustive" death in excited patients. *Psychiatr. Q.* 12:282–293, 1938.
11. Stefan, H. Sudden death of psychiatric patients following great excitation and exhaustion which has no actual anatomical basis. *Dtsch. Med. Webnschr.* 60:1550–1558, 1934. Cited by Shulack, N.R. Sudden "exhaustive" death in excited patients. *Psychiatr. Q.* 12:282, 1938.
12. Shulack, N.R. Sudden "exhaustive" death in excited patients. *Psychiatr. Q.* 18:3–12, 1944.
13. Adland, M.L. Review, case studies, therapy, and interpretation of the acute exhaustive psychoses. *Psychiatr. Q.* 21:38–69, 1947.
14. Cancro, R. The introduction of neuroleptics: a psychiatric revolution. *Psychiatr. Serv.* 51(3):333–335, 2000.
15. Lehmann, H.E. and Ban, T.A. The history of the psychopharmacology of schizophrenia. *Can. J. Psychiatr.* 42:152–162, 1997.
16. Lieberman, J.A., Golden, R., Stroup, S., and McEnvoy, J. Drugs of the psychopharmacological revolution in clinical psychiatry. *Psychiatr. Serv.* 51(10):1254–1258, 2000.
17. Wetli, C.V., Mash, D., and Karch, S.B. Cocaine-associated agitated delirium and the neuroleptic malignant syndrome. *Am. J. Emerg. Med.* 14(4):425–428, 1996.
18. Ruttenber, A.J., Lawler-Heavner, J., Yin, M., Wetli, C.V., Hearn, W.L., and Mash, D.C. Fatal excited delirium following cocaine use: epidemiologic findings provide new evidence for mechanisms of cocaine toxicity. *J. Forensic Sci.* 42(1):25–31, 1997.
19. Ruttenber, A.J., McAnally, H., and Wetli, C.V. Cocaine-associated rhabdomyolysis and excited delirium: different stages of the same syndrome. *Am. J. Forensic Med. Pathol.* 20(2):120–127, 1999.

20. Karch, S.B. and Stephens, B.G. Drug abusers who die during arrest or in custody. *J. R. Soc. Med.* 92:110–113, 1999.

21. Karch, S.B. *Karch's Pathology of Drug Abuse.* CRC Press, Boca Raton, FL, 2002.

22. Weiss, E.M., Altimari, D., Blint, D.F., and Megan, K. Deadly restraint: a *Hartford Courant* investigative report. *Hartford Courant,* October 11–15, 1998.

23. Freedman, R. Drug therapy: schizophrenia (review article). *N. Engl. J Med.* 349:1738–1749, 2003.

24. Laborit cited by Lehmann, H.E. and Ban, T.A. The history of the psychopharmacology of schizophrenia. *Can. J. Psychiatr.* 42:152–162, 1997.

25. O'Halloran, R.L. and Frank, J.G. Asphyxial death during prone restraint position revisited: a report of 21 cases. *Am. J. Forensic Med. Pathol.* 21(1):39–52, 2000.

26. Reay, D.T. and Eisele, J.W. Death from law enforcement neck holds. *Am. J Forensic Med. Pathol.* 3(3):253–258, 1982.

27. Reay, D.T., Howard, J.D., Fligner, C.L., and Ward, R.J. Effects of positional restraint on oxygen saturation and heart rate following exercise. *Am. J. Forensic Med. Pathol.* 9(1):16–18. 1988.

28. Chan, T.C., Vilke, G.N., Neuman, T., and Clausen, J.L. Restraint position and positional asphyxia. *Ann. Emerg. Med.* 30:578–586, 1997.

29. Reay, D.J., Fligner, C.L., Stilwell, A.D., and Arnold, J. Positional asphyxia during law enforcement transport. *Am. J. Forensic Med. Pathol.* 13:90–97, 1992.

30. San Diego Police Department, Final Report of the Custody Task Force, 1992.

31. O'Halloran, R.L. and Lewman, L.V. Restraint asphyxiation in excited delirium. *Am. J. Forensic Med. Pathol.* 14:289–295, 1993.

32. Stratton, S.J., Rogers, C., and Green, K. Sudden death in individuals in hobble restraints during paramedic transport. *Ann. Emerg. Med.* 25(5):710–712, 1995.

33. Farnham, F.R. and Kennedy, H.G. Acute excited states and sudden death: much journalism, little evidence. *Br. Med. J.* 315(7116):1107–1108, 1997.

34. Pollanen, M., Chiasson, D.A., and Cairns, J.T. Unexpected death related to restraint for excited delirium: a retrospective study of deaths in police custody and in the community. *Can. Med. Assoc. J.* 158(12):1603–1607, 1998.

35. Stratton, S.J., Rogers, C., Brickett, K., and Gruzinski, G. Factors associated with sudden death of individuals requiring restraint for excited delirium. *Am. J. Emerg. Med.* 19(3):187–191, 2001.

36. Flegal, K.M., Carroll, M.D., Ogden, C.L., and Johnson, C.L. Prevalence and trends in obesity among U.S. adults, 1992–2000. *J. Am. Med. Assoc.* 288(14):1723–1727, 2002.

37. Park, K.S., Korn, C.S., and Henderson, S.O. Agitated delirium and sudden death: two case reports. *Prehosp. Emerg. Care.* 5(2):214–216, 2001.

38. Vilke, G.M. and Chan, T.C. Agitated delirium and sudden death (letter to the editor). *Prehosp. Emerg. Care.* 6(2):259, 2002.

39. Henderson, S.O. and Korn, C.S. In reply. 6(2):259, 2002; 6(2):259–260, 2002.

40. Chan, T.C., Neuman, T., Clausen, J., Eisele, J., and Vilke, G.M. Weight force during prone restraint and respiratory function. *Am. J. Forensic Med. Pathol.* 25(3):185–189, 2004.

3

TRADITIONAL EXPLANATIONS FOR DEATH DUE TO EXCITED DELIRIUM SYNDROME

Traditionally, two explanations have been put forth to explain deaths due to excited delirium syndrome. One is that death is the result of positional or restraint asphyxia, the other that the death results from use of a neck hold. The authors feel that neither of these propositions explains most deaths associated with excited delirium syndrome.

Let us review what transpires during an episode of excited delirium. An individual develops a disturbance in thought, behavior, and mood and becomes agitated and violent. The excited delirium progresses to a point that police or medical personnel feel that the individual is a danger to himself or herself or to others. Police officers have a number of courses of action to pursue. Initially, they will attempt to reason with or "talk down" the individual. In former years, if the individual could not be talked down, it was not uncommon for the police to club the individual into unconsciousness Nowadays, if it is elected to use force, the police will first try to incapacitate the individual with chemical sprays such as pepper spray. Unfortunately, many individuals in the throes of excited delirium appear to be resistant to the actions of these chemical sprays. The next option is to put the individual in physical restraint. The police will attempt to grab the individual, and handcuff the individual with the hands behind the back. This usually elicits a violent struggle. During the struggle, the officers may inadvertently place an arm around the neck or try to apply a neck hold either to incapacitate the individual or to restrain the person while handcuffs are applied. Almost inevitably, as a consequence of the struggle, the individual is brought to the ground — usually prone. The struggle will continue on the ground with the individual bucking, twisting, kicking, and trying to bite.

Medical personnel will hold the arms and legs down, sometimes partly lying over the shoulders to prevent bucking. Medication will then be injected, usually intramuscularly.[1-4] The police, of course, are not able to administer drugs. In addition, the police often do not have the manpower to effect immediate restraint of an individual. The recommended minimum number of medical personnel to physically restrain an individual in excited delirium is six.[5] The lack of personnel tends to result in a more prolonged struggle than would occur in a medical institution. The police will attempt to handcuff the individual. Because individuals have to be handcuffed with their hands behind them, they must be held prone during the struggle. After placing handcuffs, the individual usually continues to struggle, thrashing about and kicking out with the feet. The police will then usually place restraints on the ankles. As police officers attempt to hold the individual down to apply handcuffs and place ankle restraints, they often place pressure on the back using their knees or by lying on the individual. After being restrained, the individual may either immediately cease struggling or continue to struggle for a short time. Following the cessation of the struggle, the individual is generally ignored until suddenly it is realized that he or she is not breathing. This usually occurs immediately after or within a few minutes following cessation of the struggle. Resuscitation is attempted and is unsuccessful.[6]

Medical personnel, following the injection, continue manual restraint until the sedative attributes of the medication become effective. Just as in the case with the police, after holding the individual down manually for a short time, struggling ceases. Usually, a minute or two later someone realizes that the patient has arrested. Even in a medical environment, resuscitation is almost uniformly unsuccessful.

There are variations on the aforementioned scenarios. In some cases, the individual arrests during the struggle before physical restraint is either applied or completed. While most individuals suffer a cardiopulmonary arrest within a few minutes following cessation of their struggling, in others the arrest is delayed. Individuals may arrest in the vehicle transporting them to jail or a hospital or on arrival at an emergency room.[7] Rarely, the individual arrests a few hours after the struggle while still being restrained in a jail, hospital, or institution.

The layperson or even the forensic pathologist reading the account of an attempt to restrain an individual in excited delirium, whether the individuals attempting restraint are police or medical personnel, has no concept of the violence with which such individuals can struggle. Thus, it is easy to be critical of police and medical personnel. Nursing protocols recommend a *minimum* of six personnel to physically restrain an individual in the throes of excited delirium.[5] In the case of a 13-year-old girl under the care of one of the authors (T.D.), four large individuals were needed to restrain the child while the author gave an injection of Haldol®.

MEDICAL EXAMINER

Prior to performing an autopsy, the medical examiner will attempt to obtain a history on the deceased as well as a detailed account of the circumstances surrounding the incident. This includes the actions of all individuals involved and whether any medications were administered before or after the arrest. If the individual dies in a hospital or institution, complete medical records should be requested as well as any original blood dating back to the time of admission. In virtually all cases, there will be a history of chronic drug abuse and/or mental illness. When an autopsy is performed, the only findings are minor injuries. Any natural disease found is usually felt to be inadequate to explain the death. It is at this time that the death is often ascribed to positional or restraint asphyxia or use of a "choke hold."[7–15] This occurs even when there is neither physical nor testimonial evidence of these having occurred or when the alleged asphyxial episode was of too short a duration to cause death. Toxicology testing on the individuals with no history of mental disease almost invariably reveals the presence of cocaine or methamphetamine, rarely other stimulants or alcohol. In the case of individuals with a mental history, many of them are found to be taking medications that have the potential of producing a fatal cardiac arrhythmia. The medical examiner should never issue a ruling regarding cause of death until the examiner is cognizant of all the facts surrounding the death, has performed a complete autopsy, and has completed all toxicological testing.

POSITIONAL/RESTRAINT ASPHYXIA

Acceptance of the concept of positional or restraint asphyxia as the cause of death in a restraint-associated death often involves suspension of common sense and logical thinking. Originally, deaths in association with excited delirium syndrome and ascribed to positional asphyxia involved individuals either placed in a situation where respiration was impaired by a compressive force on the abdomen or tied up in a way alleged to restrict respiration, and thus oxygenation of blood, e.g., hog-tying.[10–14] The former concept has some legitimacy. Thus, an individual restrained and placed in the back of a car such that the abdomen is over the transmission hump is probably a true example of positional asphyxia.[12] Even in these cases, however, it was stated that drugs were usually present in such individuals and contributed to the death.

Almost immediately after the concept of positional asphyxia was offered, the concept was expanded such that whenever anyone is restrained and dies, positional or restraint asphyxia is said to be the cause of death whatever the position of the deceased, the method of restraint, or the presence of drugs. In spite of the work of Chan et al.,[16] which essentially disproved the concept of positional asphyxia proposed up to that time, many individuals still cling to this essentially discredited concept. This is not to say that positional asphyxia cannot be a cause of death in association with excited delirium syndrome. Rather, it is a rare occurrence usually involving unusual positioning of the individual, e.g. an obese individual, hog-tied and wedged between the front and backseat of a vehicle with the abdomen draped over the transmission hump. Rarely, deaths in association with excited delirium syndrome may be due to traumatic asphyxia. This occurs if a number of individuals lie or sit on an individual for several minutes, compressing the chest and abdomen, such that respiration is not possible. Whether an extremely obese individual, lying prone, handcuffed, and with bound feet has significant impairment in the ability to oxygenate blood is not clear. A number of factors would have to be considered, including the degree of obesity.

Chan et al.[16] conducted a series of experiments to determine if placing an individual prone in the hog-tied position, following strenuous exercise, produced restriction in ventilation such that there was impairment in oxygenation of blood. They found that while this resulted in restrictive pulmonary functioning as measured by pulmonary function tests (PFT), the changes were not clinically relevant. There was no evidence of hypoxia in the restraint position after exercise, as well as no evidence of hyper-capnia either during exercise or in restraint.

In an attempt to counter Chan et al.'s work and maintain the concept of positional/restraint asphyxia, some investigators now claim that the death is due to compromise in ventilation occurring when an officer or medical worker, attempting to restrain individuals, kneels on them or lies across their backs in an attempt to prevent further struggle. Of course, as usual, no scientific backing is given for this theory. Chan et al. address this theory in a paper published in 2004.[17] They conducted a study in which weights were applied to individuals restrained in the hog-tied or hobble position, a position rarely used nowadays and the most extreme of the restraint positions. The authors utilized three positions: sitting; hog-tied with 25 lb on the back, and hog-tied with 50 lb on the back. They found that the hog-tied position, with or without 25 and 50 lb of weight force, while producing a restrictive pulmonary function pattern, did not produce any evidence of hypoxia or hypoventilation, i.e., no evidence of hypoxia, oxygen desaturation, hypercapnia, or CO_2 retention. Thus, there is no proof that the force placed on individuals by kneeling on them or lying across their bodies compromises respiration. In fact, these actions are performed daily by police making arrests of violent individuals and medical personnel restraining violent individuals without any untoward results.

NECK HOLDS

If positional/restraint asphyxia cannot be used to explain the death, then use of a neck hold is invoked as the cause of death. These allegations are often made when there is neither physical nor testimonial evidence of a hold being applied. It is just stated that the police or medical personnel are lying, as are the witnesses. When absence of trauma to the neck occurs with such allegations, it is explained that that this "proves" the neck hold was an expertly applied carotid sleeper hold. What is ignored is that use of a neck hold is manual strangulation. Death in manual strangulation is due to prolonged pressure on the neck causing complete occlusion of the carotid arteries with resultant irreversible hypoxic injury to the brain.[18]

There are two types of neck holds: the choke hold and the carotid sleeper hold.[18] Although these terms are often used interchangeably, in fact they refer to different holds whose purpose is to produce transient cerebral ischemia and unconsciousness. With both holds, the arm and forearm are used to compress the neck and thus the carotid arteries. Occasionally, a baton, a large metal flashlight, or some other object will be used to compress the neck. Use of these implements may produce extensive hemorrhage in the neck and fracture of the hyoid or larynx.

Compression of the airway usually does not occur and is not necessary for either of these holds to be effective. What is desired is compression of the carotid arteries. Two-thirds to three-quarters of the blood supply to the brain is provided by the carotid arteries with the remainder supplied by the vertebral arteries. Compression of the carotid arteries for 10 to 15 seconds produces cerebral hypoxia and loss of consciousness.[18]

The carotid arteries are easily compressed by direct pressure to the front of the neck.[18] The amount of pressure necessary to occlude the carotid arteries is approximately 11 lb. The jugular veins, adjacent to the carotid arteries, require only 4.4 lb of pressure to compress them. If the carotid arteries are continuously occluded for 2 or more minutes, on release of the pressure on the neck, respiration will usually not return spontaneously. The individual, however, should respond to cardiopulmonary resuscitation.

With choke holds the forearm is placed straight across the front of the neck.[18] The free hand grips the wrist, pulling it backward, displacing the tongue rearward with occlusion of the hypopharynx and compressing the carotid arteries. Loss of consciousness is caused by compression of the carotid arteries. If too much force is used, there can be fracture of the larynx or hyoid. Reported fractures are unilateral and involve the greater cornu of the thyroid cartilage.[18] Following loss of consciousness, the choke hold is released and the victim should regain consciousness within 20 to 30 seconds. There should be no permanent sequelae.

In the carotid sleeper hold, symmetrical pressure is supplied by the forearm and upper arm to the front of the neck such that there is compression only of the carotid arteries and jugular veins and not the airways. The arm is placed about the neck with the antecubital fossa or "crook of the arm" centered at the midline of the neck. The free hand grasps the wrist of the other arm pulling it backward, creating a "pincher" effect. This produces transient cerebral ischemia. The carotid sleeper hold impedes blood flow in the carotid arteries by pressure exerted on both sides of the neck due to the "pincher" effect of the arm and forearm. When properly applied, loss of consciousness occurs in approximately 10 to 15 seconds. On relaxation of the hold, cerebral blood flow is restored, and consciousness returns in approximately 20 seconds without any serious side effects.

If the carotid arteries are continuously occluded for 2 or more minutes, on release of the pressure on the neck, respiration will usually not return spontaneously. The individual, however, should respond to cardiopulmonary resuscitation. But, as we have seen, even in instances where emergency medical personnel witness the cardiopulmonary arrest, resuscitation is unsuccessful.[6] If most of these individuals were elderly or had severe underlying cardiovascular disease, then an argument could be made that this is the explanation for the failure to recover. Most individuals, however, are young and relatively healthy.

Thus, to kill someone with a neck hold, pressure has to be continuously applied on the neck, obstructing the carotid arteries, for 2 or more minutes. This is a relatively long time and is virtually always inconsistent with the timeline of the incident given by the witnesses. When this is pointed out, it is then alleged that there was a vasovagal reflex with cardiac arrest. Of course, there is no way to prove or disprove this contention since there would be no physical findings if this occurred. What is conveniently ignored is that there is no proof that this fatal reflex occurs in the population dying of excited delirium syndrome. Deaths in the literature referring to this concept involve elderly individuals with advanced cardiovascular disease.[19]

Because maintenance of a "choke" or "carotid" artery hold would produce death by manual strangulation, one would expect petechiae of the conjunctiva and or sclera in deaths due to excited delirium syndrome.

In fact, in deaths due to excited delirium syndrome, the presence of conjunctival and scleral petechiae is at best uncommon. In ordinary strangulation, petechiae are found in 89% of cases.[20] Pressure to the neck in manual strangulation causes complete obstruction of the carotid arteries and the adjacent jugular veins. The vertebral arteries are not affected. The petechiae are caused by rupture of venules and capillaries secondary to increased intravascular pressure as a result of obstruction of the venous return (jugular veins), in conjuncture with incomplete arterial obstruction, which permits the vertebral arteries to continue supplying some blood to the brain. Petechiae are not, however, pathognomonic of asphyxial deaths. They are seen in other diseases, e.g., acute heart failure, and may also be seen in conjunction with severe vomiting or coughing. Petechiae may form in the eyes postmortem if the individual remains face down for a prolonged period of time. The presence of "petechiae" of the mucosa of the epiglottis or larynx is not diagnosis of strangulation or any specific form of asphxyia.[18]

In some deaths due to excited delirium syndrome, hemorrhage in the neck or fractures of the hyoid or larynx is found. This is said to be "proof" that the individual died of a neck hold. What is conveniently ignored is that these injuries are merely "markers" of force applied to the neck.[18] They indicate that either pressure has been applied or a blow delivered to the neck. The injuries present, either hemorrhage or fractures, are not in themselves the cause of death.

Resuscitative injuries of the pharynx and larynx secondary to intubation can mimic injuries caused by strangulation and neck holds. Thus, in a study of 50 individuals who had endotracheal intubation prior to reaching an emergency room, 74% (34) had injuries of the airway.[21] There were injuries to the mouth consisting of focal contusions lacerations, and abrasions of the lips and buccal mucosa. In addition, there were injuries of the posterior oral pharynx and laryngopharynx consisting of contusions of the base of the tongue, the epiglottis, and the piriform recesses as well as laceration of the epiglottis. Injuries to the larynx included contusions and petechiae of the mucosa as well as hemorrhages in the superficial and deep muscles of the larynx. Externally, 2 individuals had abrasions of the skin of the neck, 3 facial petechiae, and 10 conjunctival petechiae. The occurrence of the petechiae was ascribed to chest compression during resuscitation.

The relative benign nature of neck holds is confirmed by the experience of individuals practicing the sport of judo.[22,23] In judo, choke holds known as *shime-waza* are used. Pressure is applied to the neck by the forearm, occluding the carotid arteries. Unconsciousness occurs in approximately 10 seconds. Upon release of the pressure, the individual regains consciousness in 10 to 20 seconds. Tachycardia and transient hypertension, with a rise of 30 to 40 mm Hg, may occur. Blood pressure returns to normal 3 to 4 min after release of pressure. In some cases, bradycardia and hypotension occur, presumably due to stimulation of the carotid sinus. If neck holds are inherently dangerous, then deaths should be common in practitioners of judo. Koiwai reported in 1987 that he could not find any deaths due to *shime-waza* from the inception of judo in 1882.[22]

VASOVAGAL REACTIONS (REFLEX CARDIAC DEATH)

Occasionally, it is claimed that the death of the healthy individual, following transient pressure applied to the neck, is due to a vasovagal reaction from stimulation of the carotid sinuses, i.e., a reflex cardiac death. While an interesting theory, this concept is not proved by objective evidence. The carotid sinus is a focal area of enlargement of the common carotid artery where it bifurcates into the external and internal carotids. Compression or stimulation of the carotid sinuses causes an increase in blood pressure in these sinuses with resultant slowing of the heart rate, dilation of blood vessels, and a falling blood pressure.

In normal individuals, pressure on the carotid sinus produces minimal effects with a mild decrease in heart rate (bradycardia) of less than 6 beats/minute and only a slight, insignificant, reduction in blood pressure (less then 10 mm Hg).[19] Some individuals, however, have an extreme reaction to stimulation of the carotid sinuses. In individuals with a hyperactive/hypersensitive carotid sinus, i.e., carotid sinus syndrome, there is an exaggeration of the normal response with syncope and marked hypotension occurring. Occasional deaths have been referenced.[24] Review of the original literature in regard to the alleged deaths, however, reveals that the individuals dying all had serious underlying cardiovascular disease which in itself could explain death.

Carotid sinus syndrome is diagnosed in a symptomatic individual when carotid sinus stimulation produces asystole exceeding 3 seconds or a fall in systolic blood pressure exceeding 50 mm Hg or a combination of the two. It is found in older individuals. Hyperactive carotid sinus reflex is not a part of the normal aging process, however.[25,26] Parry et al.[27] studied 25 healthy individuals older than 55 years of age. Carotid sinus stimulation in both the supine and upright positions failed to reveal significant cardioinhibitory response (asystole exceeding 3 seconds). Another study of 25 subjects, ages 61 to 87 by McIntosh et al.[25] found that none of the subjects had asystole of 3 seconds or more. In regard to a significant decrease in systolic blood pressure (a 50 mm Hg fall) in reaction to the stimulation, only three tested positive; these patients were asymptomatic.

In a study of 21 patients with carotid sinus hyperactivity, only two did not have cardiac disease.[28] One was 50 years old; the other 76 years, hardly the typical age for excited delirium syndrome victims. Even then, the author admitted that organic heart disease had not been completely ruled out in these two individuals.

Thus, we can see that carotid sinus syndrome is found in older individuals with underlying coronary atherosclerosis or hypertensive cardiovascular disease.[28] To ascribe death to carotid sinus stimulation in cases of excited delirium syndrome is at best tenuous, as individuals dying of excited delirium syndrome are not elderly with cardiovascular disease.

OLERESIN CAPSICUM

Oleresin capsicum or pepper spray canisters consist of a carrier (water or alcohol) for the capsacinoids (the active ingredients), a propellant, and an aerosol valve nozzle. The concentration of capsacinoids varies from 1% in canisters intended for the public to 5 to 10% in canisters for police. Oleresin capsicum is the active ingredient in pepper spray. It is an extract of the pepper plant of genus capsicum, consisting of a complex mixture of capsacinoids. These compounds stimulate chemo-nociceptors in nerve endings producing pain and burning sensations of the skin, eyes, nose, and oropharynx. Inhalation results in coughing, gagging, blepharospasm with involuntary closure of the eyes, bronchoconstriction, mucus secretion, shortness of breath, and inability to speak. In the lungs, oleresin capsicum spray produces depletion of neurotransmitters of the sensory nerves with resultant activation of mast cells and release of histamine.[29] The effects of oleresin capsicum spray result in an inability to fight or resist in most individuals, thus the employment of oleresin capsicum spray by police. The effects disappear in 20 to 30 minutes. In a number of cases investigated by one of the authors (V.J.M.D.), individuals experiencing excited delirium were found to be completely resistant to repeated spraying with oleresin capsicum, with no discernible effect on the individuals.

Following its widespread use by police, a number of deaths associated with oleresin capsicum spray use began to be reported.[30–32] Review of these cases fails to reveal any evidence conclusively linking oleresin capsicum spray with a role in the death. Virtually all these individuals were in the throes of excited delirium at the time of spraying, with toxicological analysis revealing the presence of cocaine or methamphetamine. Individuals free of drugs of abuse inevitably give a history of a psychotic disease.

Some individuals have suggested that oleresin capsicum spray can cause death by laryngospasm and bronchoconstriction.[30] Tests appear to disprove this contention. Chan et al.[33] conducted a series of experiments to determine the effect of oleresin capsicum spray on respiratory function.

In this study, 35 volunteers were exposed to oleresin capsicum or placebo spray, followed by 10 minutes of sitting or prone maximal restraint position (PMRP), i.e., hog-tying. During this 10-minute interval, spirometry, oximetry, and endtidal CO_2 levels were collected and compared between the groups and with normal values. In both the sitting and restraint positions, exposure to oleresin capsicum did not result in any significant differences between the oleresin capsicum and placebo groups. Spirometric measurements remained in the normal ranges. There was no evidence of hypoxemia or hypoventilation.

TASERS

The newest device used by police in their encounters with individuals in excited delirium is the Taser. Tasers are handheld devices that fire two fish-hook-like barbed darts attached to wires up to a distance of 21 feet (an interchangeable 15-foot cartridge is available). The darts are designed to penetrate up to 2 inches of clothing or skin. Penetration of skin is not necessary for the Taser to work, however. The Taser is most effective when both darts lodge in or on the body. A high-voltage (50,000 volt), low amperage (162 mA) current is delivered down the insulated, copper-clad, steel wires to the target. Wattage is 26 watts; energy 1.76 joules. Tasers are manufactured by Taser International, an Arizona-based company. The current model, the M 26, was introduced in 1999. In 2003, a new model, the Taser X26, was introduced. It is smaller and lighter than the M26 but has the same voltage. The electrical pulse causes uncontrollable contraction of the muscles and immediate collapse. The shocks can be repeated. The darts are propelled by a cartridge of compressed nitrogen.

Just as deaths in excited delirium have been ascribed to choke holds, restraint asphyxia, and the use of pepper spray, they are now being blamed on the use of Tasers.[34,35] The *Arizona Republic* reported on 90 deaths following the use of the Taser from 1999 to 2005.[34] Amnesty International mentions "more than 70" deaths since 2001 and reviewed 74.[35] On reviewing the details of these deaths, almost invariably they describe individuals in excited delirium, high on illegal stimulants who die not at the time they are "Tasered" but sometime after, usually during the "period of peril." If death is due to ventricular fibrillation or asystole produced by the Taser pulse, then the individual would lose consciousness immediately (3 to 4 seconds up to a maximum of 10 to 15 seconds). This does not seem to be occurring in the vast majority, if not virtually all, of the cases. Death in these cases seems to be, in virtually all instances, due to the excited delirium syndrome.

EXPLAINING EXCITED DELIRIUM SYNDROME

To this point, we have said what is not causing death in excited delirium syndrome. What then is? It is the authors' contention that death is due to a combination of the normal physiologic changes seen in a struggle, combined with, depending on the case, the use of illicit drugs, medications, and natural disease. The next chapter discusses the normal physiologic reaction to stress, which can turn lethal. Chapter 5 shows how drugs, both illegal and medicinal, can accentuate normal physiological reactions turning them lethal.

REFERENCES

1. Brice, J.H., Pirrallo, R.G., Racht, E., Zachariah, B.S., and Krohmer, J. Management of the violent patient. *Prehosp. Emerg. Care* 7(1):48–55, 2002.
2. Currier, G.W. and Allen, M.H. Physical and chemical restraint in the psychiatric emergency service. *Psychiatr. Serv.* 51(6):717–719, 2000.
3. Binder, R.L. and McNiel, D.E. Emergency psychiatry: contemporary practices in managing acutely violent patients in 20 psychiatric emergency rooms. *Psychiatr. Serv.* 50:1553–1554, 1999.
4. Citrome, L. and Volavka, J. Violent patients in the emergency setting. *Psychiatr. Clin. North Am.* 22(4):789–801, 1999.
5. Farrell, S.P., Harmon, R.B., and Hastings, S. Nursing management of acute psychotic episodes. *Nursing Clin. North Am.* 33(1):187–200, 1998.
6. Stratton, S.J., Rogers, C., Brickett, K., and Gruzinski, G. Factors associated with sudden death of individuals requiring restraint for excited delirium. *Am. J. Emerg. Med.* 19(3):187–191, 2001.
7. Ross, D.L. Factors associated with excited delirium deaths in police custody. *Mod. Path*ol. 11(11):1127–1137, 1998.
8. Reay, D.T. and Eisele, J.W. Death from law enforcement neck holds. *Am. J Forensic Med. Pathol.* 3(3):253–258, 1982.
9. Kornblum, R.N. Medical analysis of police choke holds and general neck trauma. I and II. *Trauma* 27:7–60; 28:13–64, 1986.
10. Stratton, S.J., Rogers, C., and Green, K. Sudden death in individuals in hobble restraints during paramedic transport. *Ann. Emerg. Med.* 25(5):710–712, 1995.
11. Reay, D.T., Howard, J.D., Fligner, C.L., and Ward, R.J. Effects of positional restraint on oxygen saturation and heart rate following exercise. *Am. J. Forensic Med. Pathol.* 9(1):16–18, 1988.
12. Reay, D.T., Fligner, C.L., Stilwell, A.D., and Arnold, J. Positional asphyxia during law enforcement transport. *Am. J. Forensic Med. Pathol.* 13(2):90–97, 1992.
13. O'Halloran, R.L. and Lewman, L.V. Restraint asphyxiation in excited delirium. *Am. J. Forensic Med. Pathol.* 14(4):289–295, 1993.
14. O'Halloran, R.L. and Frank, J.G. Asphyxial death during prone restraint position revisited: a report of 21 cases. *Am. J. Forensic Med. Pathol.* 21(1):39–52, 2000.
15. Pollanen, M., Chiasson, D.A., and Cairns, J.T. Unexpected death related to restraint for excited delirium: a retrospective study of deaths in police custody and in the community. *Can. Med. Assoc. J.* 158(12):1603–1607, 1998.

16. Chan, T.C., Vilke, G.N., Neuman, T., and Clausen, J.L. Restraint position and positional asphyxia. *Ann. Emerg. Med.* 30:578–586, 1997.

17. Chan, T.C., Neuman, T., Clausen, J., Eisele, J., and Vilke, G.M. Weight force during prone restraint and respiratory function. *Am. J. Forensic Med. Pathol.* 25:185–189, 2004.

18. Di Maio, V.J.M. and Di Maio, D.J. *Forensic Pathology,* 2nd ed. CRC Press. Boca Raton, FL, 2001.

19. Weiss, S. and Baker, J.P. The carotid sinus reflex in health and disease. *Medicine* 12:297–354, 1933.

20. Di Maio, V.J.M. Homicidal asphyxia. *Am. J. Forensic Med. Pathol.* 21(1):1–4, 2000.

21. Raven, K.P., Reay, D.T., and Harruff, R.C. Artifactual injuries of the larynx produced by resuscitative intubation. *Am. J. Forensic Med. Pathol.* 20(1):31–36, 1999.

22. Koiwai, E.K. Deaths allegedly caused by the use of "choke holds" (*Shime-Waza*). *J. Forensic Sci.* 32(2):419–432, 1987.

23. Ikai, M., Ishiko, T., Ueda, G. et al. Physiological studies on "choking" in judo. *Bull. Assoc. Sci. Stud. Judo. Report 1.* 1–22, 1958.

24. Thomas, J.E. Hyperactive carotid sinus reflexes and carotid sinus syncope. *Mayo Clin. Proc.* 44:127–139, 1969.

25. McIntosh, S.J., Lawson, J., and Kenny, R.A. Heart rate and blood pressure responses to carotid massage in healthy elderly subjects. *Age Aging* 23:57–61, 1994.

26. McIntosh, S.J., Lawson, J., and Kenny, R.A. Clinical characteristic of vasode-pressor, cardio-inhibitory, and mixed carotid sinus syndrome in the elderly. *Am. J. Med.* 95(2):203–208, 1993.

27. Parry, S.W., Richardson, D.A., O'Shea, D.B., and Kenny, R.A. Diagnosis of carotid sinus hypersensitivity in older adults: carotid sinus massage in the upright position is essential. *Heart* 83(1):22–23, 2000.

28. Walter, P.F., Crawley, I.S., and Dorney, E.R. Carotid sinus hypersensitivity and syncope. *Am. J. Cardiol.* 42:396–403, 1978.

29. Busker, R.W. and van Helden, H.P.M. Toxicologic examination of pepper spray as a possible weapon for the Dutch police. *Am. J. Forensic Med Pathol.* 19(4):309–316, 1998.

30. Granfield, J., Onnen, J., and Petty, C.S. Pepper spray and in-custody deaths. Executive Brief. Science & Technology. International Association of Chiefs of Police, Washington, D.C., 1994.

31. Steffee, C.H., Lantz, P.E., Flannagan, L.M. et al. Oleoresin capsicum (pepper) spray and "in-custody deaths." *Am. J. Forensic Med Pathol.* 16(3):185–192, 1995.

32. Bunting, S. First death attributed to OC occurs in North Carolina. *ASLET J.* 13–16, 1993.

33. Chan, T.C., Vilke, G.M., Clausen, J., Clark, R.F., Schmidt, P., Snowden, T., and Neuman, T. The effect of oleoresin capsicum "pepper spray" inhalation on respiratory function. *J. Forensic Sci.* 47(2):299–304, 2002.

34. Anglen, R. 90 cases of death following stun-gun use. *Arizona Republic,* January 26, 2005.

35. Amnesty International. Excessive and lethal force? Amnesty International's concerns about deaths and ill-treatment involving police use of Tasers. *AI Index;* AMR 51/139/2004. November 30, 2004.

4

PHYSIOLOGICAL REACTIONS TO STRESS

The previous chapters discussed the history of excited delirium syndrome, its presentation, and traditional theories to explain the deaths occurring in this entity. If the cause of such deaths is not positional/restraint asphyxia or choke holds, what is the cause? It is the authors' contention that death is due to a combination of the normal physiologic changes seen in a struggle, combined with, depending on the case, the use of illicit drugs, medications, and natural disease. In some individuals, polymorphism of cardiac adrenoreceptors with resultant exacerbation of the normal responses to violent physical activity may also play a role. This chapter discusses the sympathetic nervous system and the normal physiologic changes that occur during and following strenuous physical activity, e.g., struggle, relating them to deaths due to excited delirium syndrome. Chapter 5 discusses the actions of illegal stimulants, such as cocaine and meth-amphetamine, and psychiatric medications on the nervous and cardiovas-cular systems.

THE SYMPATHETIC NERVOUS SYSTEM

The sympathetic nervous system is the controller of the "fight or flight" response. Whenever an individual is exposed to stress, there is a wide-spread physiological reaction throughout the body.[1] The stress can be exogenous or endogenous; physical or psychological. The reaction of the body to stress is integrated in the brain through the hypothalamus.[1-3] With stimulation of the hypothalamus, signals are transmitted downward through the reticular formation of the brain stem to the autonomic control centers and into the spinal cord, producing massive sympathetic discharge.

The motor component of the sympathetic nervous system is a two neuron system consisting of pre- and postganglionic neurons. The preganglionic neurons are located in the spinal cord from T1–L2. Axons from these preganglionic neurons leave the cord and synapse with neurons in the paravertebral regions forming paravertebral ganglias. The postganglion neurons in the paravertebral ganglias then send axons from the ganglia to organs. It is these postganglion neurons that are of most concern here.

Neurons

Neurons (nerve cells) consist of a cell body, which contains the nucleus; dendrites, which are branched processes, extending from the cell body, that receive chemical messages from other neurons; and the axon. The axon is a process extending from the cell body that carries chemical messages from the cell body to the synapse. Neurons are not physically continuous with each other or with the organs that they innervate. The region or cleft between connecting neurons, as well as connecting neurons and organs, is called the *synapse* (Figure 4.1). Transmission of nerve impulses from nerve to nerve, or nerve to organ, is accomplished by release of neurotransmitters from the nerves into the synapses.[1-3] In the sympathetic nervous system, the preganglionic fibers release acetylcholine at the synapses, and the postganglionic fibers, i.e., those that go to organs, release norepinephrine. It is the postsynaptic synapses that are the main concern here.

Norepinephrine released from axons into the synapse interacts with specific receptors on the recipient cells known as adrenoceptors (see Figure 4.1). *Adrenoceptors* are sites on cell membranes through which norepinephrine and epinephrine act as neurotransmitters in the central nervous system, the cardiovascular system, and other organs. Adrenoceptors are present on the cell membranes of neurons, peripheral cells, and organs. The sympathetic nervous system influences the cardiovascular system through changes in the release of norepinephrine from sympathetic nerve terminals and norepinephrine and epinephrine from the adrenals, with these substances then acting on receptors on the organs or tissue.

Neurotransmitters

Neurotransmitters are chemical messengers (amino acids or biogenic amines) that travel through synapses to deliver information to other neurons or cells.[1-3] They are produced within neurons, stored in vesicles at the presynaptic terminals, and released into the synaptic clefts upon nerve stimulation (see Figure 4.1). The neurotransmitters of interest here are the catecholamines. The principal catecholamines are epinephrine,

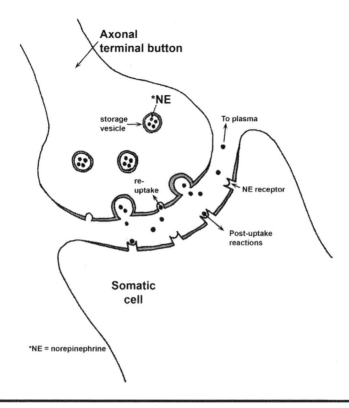

Figure 4.1 Norepinephrine (NE) released from axons into the synapse interacts with receptors on the recipient cells. The transport system facilitates the re-uptake of NE by the releasing neuron, controlling the concentration of NE, and, thus, neuronal excitation.

norepinephrine, and dopamine.[3] They are synthesized from tyrosine, an amino acid. In the production of norepinephrine from tyrosine, dopamine is an intermediary product. The principal catecholamines in the brain are norepinephrine and dopamine; outside the brain norepinephrine and epinephrine. Outside the brain, sympathetic neurons release norepinephrine and the adrenals norepinephrine and epinephrine. Neurotransmitters react with receptors on both presynaptic and postsynaptic sites.

Reuptake mechanisms, specific enzymes, or diffusion out of the synapse rapidly inactivate the neurotransmitters released into the synapse. This controls the degree of neurogenic excitation. Virtually all neurotransmitters are recaptured by transport systems, located at the nerve terminals of the releasing neurons (see Figure 4.1). Transport systems, by facilitating the rapid reuptake of neurotransmitters by the releasing neuron, control the concentration of extracellular neurotransmitters and, thus, neuronal excitation.

Neuromodulators are somewhat similar to neurotransmitters. They are secreted by neurons, stored in vesicles, and released on neural stimulation.[3] They bind to their own specific receptors and act principally by indirect means, i.e., their effects on neurotransmitters. Neurotransmitters and neuromodulators may coexist in the same neuron. Neuromodulators can inhibit or enhance the release of neurotransmitters via presynaptic receptors.

Receptors[2–5]

Most receptors are membrane-bound proteins. Receptors may be either presynaptic or postsynaptic. On binding with a neurotransmitter, there is modification of the receptor site allowing either an ion current to flow (an ionotropic receptor) or elicitation of a cascade of intracellular events (metabotropic receptor).[3] Autoreceptors are located presynaptically and may bind neurotransmitters or neuromodulators released by the presynaptic cell. Activation of auto receptors results in modulation by the feedback mechanism of the turnover of released neurotransmitters and neuromodulators.

α-Adrenoceptors[3–7]

The membrane receptors responsible for mediating responses to catecholamines were initially divided into α- and β-adrenoceptors.[1–7] α-Adrenoceptors are differentiated into α_1-adrenoceptors and α_2-adrenoceptors. *α_1-Adrenoceptors are usually postsynaptic and in effector organs while α_2-adrenoceptors are located principally presynaptically and regulate the release of norepinephrine.* α_2-Adrenoceptors, however, have been identified in both pre- and postsynaptic anatomical locations. α_1-Adrenoceptors were thought to be responsible for excitatory responses, α_2-adrenoceptors for inhibitory responses. While true in general, α_2-adrenoceptors can also mediate excitatory responses. Both α_1- and α_2-adrenoceptors can in turn be divided into three subtypes: α_{1A}, α_{1B}, α_{1D}, and α_{2A}, α_{2B}, and α_{2C} adrenoceptors.

Vascular smooth muscles possess both α- and β-adrenoceptors with α-receptors predominating.[6,7] *In the vascular system, both α_1-adrenoceptors and α_2-adrenoceptors are responsible for vasoconstriction with the α_1-adrenoceptors dominant in arteries and the α_2-adrenoceptors in veins.*[6]

β-Adrenoceptors[3–7]

There are three β-adrenoceptors: β_1, β_2, and β_3. The principal beta receptors are the β_1 and β_2 receptors. β_1- and β_2-adrenoceptors mediate the cardiovascular responses to norepinephrine released from nerve terminals and to circulating epinephrine and norepinephrine from the adrenals. *The predominant receptor in cardiac myocytes (muscle cells) is the β_1 subtype.* Catecholamines induce positive inotropic (force of contraction), chronotropic (rate), and lusitropic (relaxant) responses in the heart by way of β_1 receptors. Under normal physiologic conditions, β_2 receptors are only a minor component of catecholamine response in the heart.

Activation of beta receptors in vascular smooth muscle results in relaxation of the muscle. β_2 receptors are the predominant subtype in vascular smooth muscle. Maximum relaxation of the vessels is evoked by β_2-receptor stimulation rather than β_1. In some vessels, however, e.g., the coronary arteries, β_1 receptors predominate.

Coronary Arteries

The small coronary arteries and arterioles (diameter <300 μm) are the principal determinants of coronary artery resistance. Both α_1- and α_2-adrenoceptors mediate coronary vasoconstriction, with α_1 predominating in the larger vessels and α_2 in the microcirculation. β_1 receptors are also present in the coronary arteries.[8]

Sympathetic activation of normal coronary arteries by stress or physical activity results in vasodilatation of both epicardial and microvessels. In contrast, in the presence of atherosclerosis or endothelial dysfunction, there is vasoconstriction during exercise.[8] This can be sufficient to produce myocardial ischemia. The fact that vasoconstriction occurs in the presence of atherosclerosis or endothelial dysfunction is significant in that accelerated development of atherosclerosis and endothelial injury is produced by chronic use of cocaine and methamphetamine.[9] Individuals dying of excited delirium syndrome are typically chronic users of these stimulants. In addition, there is evidence of genetic determination of α-receptor-mediated coronary constriction, with resultant supersensitivity to α_2-receptor-mediated constriction.[8] This is due to polymorphism in a gene.

The Heart

The predominant adrenergic receptor in cardiac muscle cells (myocytes) is the β_1 subtype.[4] These receptors mediate the cardiovascular responses to norepinephrine released from nerve terminals and to circulating epinephrine and norepinephrine from the adrenals. The catecholamines induce positive inotropic, chronotropic, and lusitropic (relaxant) responses in the heart by way of the β_1 receptors. Under normal conditions, β_2 receptors are only a minor component of catecholamine response in the heart. *The action of norepinephrine on the heart is predominantly* *stimulation of the α_1 receptors in the coronary arteries and β_1 receptors in the myocytes.*

Elevated levels of catecholamines are associated with myocardial necrosis and toxic myocarditis.[10] The earliest lesions of myocardial necrosis are subendocardial and intramyocardial areas of hemorrhage, predominantly in the left ventricle. This progresses to edema, eosinophilic changes of the myofibers, myofibril degeneration, and contraction bands. A mononuclear inflammatory infiltrate and then focal myocardial fibrosis follow this. If toxic myocarditis develops, there are multiple foci of myocardial necrosis of different ages accompanied by an extensive infiltrate of polymorphonuclear leukocytes, lymphocytes, and plasma cells. This progresses to foci of proliferating fibroblasts with minimal macrophage infiltrate and foci of interstitial fibrosis.

Polymorphism

A substantial degree of polymorphism or variation occurs in genes in the general population.[11] The significance of these variants is just now being investigated. Presynaptic α_2 receptors (α_{2A}- and α_{2C}-adrenoceptors) inhibit the release of norepinephrine from cardiac sympathetic nerves via negative feedback. β_1 receptors, the predominant β receptor in cardiac cells, are responsive to circulating epinephrine and to norepinephrine released from cardiac sympathetic nerves. Activation results in increased cardiac inotropy, chronotropy, and lusitrophy.

Small et al.[12] demonstrated that in some individuals a polymorphic alpha 2c receptor (alpha 2c Del 322-325) produced a substantial loss of the normal negative feedback such that there was an increase in synaptic norepinephrine release. In addition, a variant of the β_1 receptors (beta1 Arg 389) enhances β_1-receptor activity. The combination of the two receptor variants in the same individual, resulting in an increase in norepinephrine release and enhanced β_1-receptor function at the cardiac myocyte, appeared to act synergistically to increase the risk of heart failure.

The presence of polymorphic α_2 and β_1 receptors may explain why some individuals die following the physical stress of excited delirium syndrome while the bulk of the population does not.

Adrenals

The adrenal is unusual in that preganglionic neurons go directly to the medulla of the adrenal.[1] There are no postganglionic synapses. These preganglionic fibers release acetylcholine at their junction with the adrenal medullae. Norepinephrine and epinephrine are then secreted by the adrenal medulla; 80% of the secretion is epinephrine and 20% norepinephrine. They have basically the same effect on organs that direct sympathetic stimulation does. The only difference is that the effects last five to ten times as long because these substances are slowly removed from the blood over a period of 1 to 3 minutes.

Conclusion

We can see that stimulation of the sympathetic nervous system causes release of norepinephrine at the synapses and norepinephrine and epinephrine into the blood from the adrenals.[1] The norepinephrine works on the β_1 myocytes of the heart to cause it to beat harder and faster.[4] This in turn results in a greater demand for oxygen by the myocardium. If the coronary arteries have either endothelial injury or atherosclerosis, typical complications resulting from chronic use of cocaine and methamphetamine, there will be contraction of the coronary arteries with decreased supply of oxygenated blood to the myocardium at a time when increased amounts are needed.[8,9] This predisposes to development of a cardiac arrhythmia.

PHYSIOLOGICAL EFFECTS OF STRENUOUS/VIOLENT PHYSICAL ACTIVITY

In excited delirium syndrome, death often occurs immediately after an individual is restrained and struggling ceases. This post-struggle period corresponds to the time of "post exercise peril" described by Dimsdale et al.[13] It is a time when an individual is unusually susceptible to developing a fatal cardiac arrhythmia. An understanding of the physiological changes that lead to "post exercise peril" is important to understanding excited delirium syndrome.

Dimsdale et al. found that during exercise an individual's blood norepinephrine and epinephrine increased, with norepinephrine increasing more sharply.[13] Peak levels of these catecholamines, however, did not occur during the struggle but in the 3 minutes immediately following cessation of the exercise. Following cessation of exercise, epinephrine and norepinephrine continue to rise, with norepinephrine levels more than tenfold above baseline levels and epinephrine threefold.

The catecholamines acting on the heart consist of norepinephrine from the postsynaptic neurons of the sympathetic nervous system and norepinephrine and epinephrine released from the adrenals.

The action of norepinephrine on the heart is predominantly stimulation of the α_1 and β_1 receptors. Stimulation of β_1 receptors increases heart rate, contractility, and velocity of conduction. α_1 receptors are found in the coronary arteries. Norepinephrine interacting with α_1 receptors may cause vasoconstriction, thus decreasing the amount of oxygenated blood being supplied to the myocardium at a time when an increased amount is needed due to greater demand being put on the heart resulting from the stimulation of the β_1 receptors. Constriction occurs if there is either atherosclerosis or endothelial dysfunction of the coronary vessels, a finding common in chronic abusers of stimulants.[8,9] Epinephrine interacts with all four receptors — $\alpha_1, \alpha_2, \beta_1,$ and β_2 — reinforcing the cardiac and coronary actions of norepinephrine.

Compounding the physiological actions of elevated levels of catecholamine are changes in blood potassium levels. Young et al.[14] investigated not only the relationship between stress and catecholamine levels in blood but also levels of potassium. Like Dimsdale et al., they found that the highest levels of plasma catecholamines occurred during the 3 minutes post-exercise. In their studies, epinephrine levels peaked 1 minute after cessation of exercise, at which time the mean value was more than eightfold greater than the mean resting level. Elevated epinephrine levels were present for several additional minutes with a mean value of 1½ times the resting level at 10 minutes post-exercise. For norepinephrine, 1 minute following cessation of exercise, the level was seven times greater than the resting level. At 10 minutes, the norepinephrine level was twice the resting level.

Blood potassium concentrations have a very narrow range of safety (3.5 to 5.1 mEq/l). Fatal cardiac arrhythmia is associated with both hyperkalemia and hypokalemia. Hypokalemia occurs when serum potassium is less than 3.5 mmol/l. With mild hypokalemia (serum potassium of 3.0 to 3.5 mmol/l), there are usually no symptoms.[15] Severe hypokalemia (<2.5 mmol/L) produces symptoms including muscle necrosis. Both mild and severe hypokalemia increase the incidence of cardiac arrhythmia.[15] Hypokalemia predisposes one to prolongation of the QT interval, development of torsade de pointes, and sudden cardiac death.[16]

Young et al.[14] found that during exercise the mean plasma potassium increased slightly more than 1 mEq/l. Following cessation of exercise, the potassium level fell rapidly returning to approximately normal levels in 5 minutes. The maximum rate of fall occurred within the first or second minute post-exercise.

Additional investigation on the regulation of potassium during and after exercise revealed even more dramatic changes. In some individuals engaged in strenuous exercise, plasma potassium levels of 9 mEq/l may occur if the exercise is carried to exhaustion.[17] Peak levels were proportional to the intensity of the exercise, contracting muscle mass, and duration of exercise. There is little evidence, however, that these extremely high levels of potassium due to exercise adversely affect cardiac functioning.[17,18] Such levels can only be maintained for 1 to 2 minutes before exercise has to be stopped due to exhaustion. Studies by Paterson et al.[19] and Leitch and Paterson[20] suggest that exercise-induced increases in blood catecholamines have a cardioprotective effect on hyperkalemia. Catecholamines are known activators of potassium reuptake by noncontracting tissue. Acting on β_2 receptors, they cause a shift of potassium into the cells.[15] There is no evidence, however, that catecholamines offer the same protection against hypokalemia.

While sustained submaximal exercise can produce prolonged elevations in K^+, it is felt that rather than the high levels producing cardiac arrhythmia, it is the rapid drop to low levels following cessation of exercise that produces an arrhythmia. Serum K^+ may fall to approximately 2 mEq/l within 5 minutes. This hypokalemia predisposes one to prolongation of the QT interval, development of torsade de pointes, and sudden cardiac death.

Bronchodilators such as albuterol can reduce serum potassium by producing a potassium shift into cells. "A standard dose of nebulized albuterol reduces serum potassium by 0.2 to 0.4 mmol per liter, and a second dose taken within one hour reduces it by almost 1 mmol per liter."[16] Reduction in serum potassium can be produced by theophylline and caffeine and diuretics. Severe hypokalemia can also be induced by ingestion of large amounts of verapamil.[16]

Hyperthermia is not uncommon in cases of excited delirium syndrome. The exact incidence is unknown because body temperature is often not taken if death is rapid. Victims of excited delirium syndrome have been found to have a reduction in the number of D2 receptors in the temperature regulatory centers of the hypothalamus. These receptors mediate body temperature. A reduction in their number could lead to hyperthermia.[21]

REFERENCES

1. Guyton, A.C. and Hall, J.E. *Medical Physiology,* 10th ed. W.B. Saunders, Philadelphia, 2000.
2. World Health Organization. *Neuroscience of Psychoactive Substance Use and Dependence.* WHO, Geneva, Switzerland 2004.
3. Cooper, J.R., Bloom, F.E., and Roth, R.H. *The Biochemical Basis of Neuropharmacology,* 8th ed. Oxford University Press, New York, 2003.
4. Katz, A.M. *Physiology of the Heart.* Lippincott/Williams & Wilkins, Philadelphia, 2001.
5. Insel, P.A. Seminars in medicine of the Beth Israel Hosp., Boston: Adrenergic receptors — evolving concepts and clinical implications (review article). *N. Engl. J. Med.* 334(9):580–585, 1996.
6. Calzada, B.C. and De Artinano, A.A. Alpha-adrenoceptor subtypes. *Pharm. Res.* 44(3):195–208, 2001.

7. Guimaraes, S. and Moura, D. Vascular adrenoceptors: an update. *Pharm. Rev.* 53:319–356, 2001.
8. Heusch, G., Baumgart, D., Camici, P. et al. [alpha]-Adrenergic coronary vasoconstriction and myocardial ischemia in humans. *Circulation* 101(6):689–694, 2000.
9. Lange, R.A. and Hillis, L.D. Cardiovascular complications of cocaine use. *N. Engl. J. Med.* 345(5):351–358, 2001.
10. Silver, M.D., Gotlieb, A.I., and Schoen, F.J. *Cardiovascular Pathology.* Churchill Livingstone, Philadelphia, 2001.
11. Hajjar, R.J. and MacRae, C.A. Editorial: Adrenergic-receptor polymorphism and heart failure. *N. Engl. J. Med.* 347(15):1196–1198, 2002.
12. Small, K.M., Wagoner, L.E., Levin, A.M., Kardia, S.L.R., and Liggett, S.B. Synergistic polymorphisms of B_1 and alpha $_{2c}$ adrenergic receptors and the risk of congestive heart failure. *N. Engl. J. Med.* 347(15):1135–1142, 2002.
13. Dimsdale, J.E., Hartley, G.T., Guiney, T., Ruskin, J.N., and Greenblatt, D. Postexercise peril: plasma catecholamines and exercise. *J. Am. Med. Assoc.* 251:630–632, 1984.
14. Young, D.B., Srivastava, T.N., Fitzovich, D.E., Kivlighn, S.D., and Hamaguchi, M. Potassium and catecholamine concentrations in the immediate post exercise period. *Am. J. Med. Sci.* 304:150–153, 1992.
15. Rastergar, A. and Soleimani, M. Hypokalaemia and hyperkalaemia. *Postgrad. Med. J.* 77:759–764, 2001.
16. Gennar, F.J. Current concepts: hypokalemia (review article). *N. Engl. J. Med.* 339(7):451–458, 1998.
17. Medbo, J.I. and Sejersted, O.M. Plasma potassium changes with high intensity exercise. *J. Physiol.* 421:105–122, 1990.
18. Lindinger, M.I. Potassium regulation during exercise and recovery in humans: implications for skeletal and cardiac muscle. *J. Mol. Cell. Cardiol.* 27(4):1011–1022, 1995.
19. Paterson, D.J., Rogers, J., Powell, T., and Brown, H.F. Effect of catecholamines on the ventricular myocyte action potential in raised extracellular potassium. *Acta Physiol. Scand.* 148:177–186, 1993.
20. Leitch, S.P. and Paterson, D.J. Interactive effects of K^+, acidosis, and catecholamines on isolated rabbit heart: implications for exercise. *J. Appl. Physiol.* 77(3):1164–1171, 1994.
21. Karch, S.B. *Karch's Pathology of Drug Abuse.* CRC Press, Boca Raton, FL, 2002.

5

EFFECTS OF DRUGS ON THE HEART, BRAIN, AND SYMPATHETIC NERVOUS SYSTEM

In virtually all deaths due to excited delirium syndrome, drugs, whether illicit or therapeutic, play a role. The drugs of abuse most commonly associated with excited delirium syndrome are cocaine, methamphetamine, phencyclidine (PCP), and to a lesser degree alcohol. Many of the psychotropic drugs also have a potential to contribute to the development of death due to excited delirium syndrome.

CARDIAC INJURY DUE TO CHRONIC ELEVATION OF BLOOD CATECHOLAMINE LEVELS

Cocaine and methamphetamine are cardiotoxic. These effects are a consequence of the elevated levels of catecholamines resulting from their use. The effects are dose related and usually cumulative. Thus, chronic abuse of these drugs is associated with cardiomyopathy with an increase in heart weight.[1-3] Sudden cardiac death due to arrhythmia is a known complication of cardiomyopathy and left ventricular hypertrophy.[4,5] Chronic abuse has also been linked to accelerated atherosclerosis of the coronary arteries.[6]

Elevated levels of catecholamines are associated with myocardial necrosis and toxic myocarditis.[4] The earliest lesions of myocardial necrosis are subendocardial and intra-myocardial areas of hemorrhage, predominantly in the left ventricle. This progresses to edema, eosinophilic changes of the myofibers, myofibril degeneration, and contraction bands. A mononuclear inflammatory infiltrate and then focal myocardial fibrosis follow this. If toxic myocarditis develops, there are multiple foci of myocardial necrosis of different ages accompanied by an extensive infiltrate of polymorphonuclear leukocytes, lymphocytes, and plasma cells. This progresses to foci of proliferating fibroblasts with minimal macrophage infiltrate and foci of interstitial fibrosis.

Determination that the heart is enlarged is made somewhat difficult by confusion in the literature regarding normal heart weights. In older texts, a male heart was said to weigh between 270 and 360 g, a female heart between 200 and 280 g.[7] Zeek developed a formula for determining normal heart weight utilizing height.[8] For normally nourished adult males, it is 1.9 times the body length in centimeters minus 2.1 ± 40; for females 1.78 times body length minus 21.58 ± 30.

Many current textbooks cite a study from the Mayo Clinic Rochester in determining normal heart weights.[9] This study relates heart weight predominantly to bodyweight. Using this study, virtually any heart weight is "normal" if an individual is fat enough. There are a number of problems with this study. The most obvious is that if weight determines heart size, then as one gains and loses weight the heart follows suit, going up and down like a yo-yo.

The authors favor using heart weight ranges in the older textbooks for other reasons as well. Hospitalizations at that time were much shorter as treatment was less effective. Therefore, deceased individuals were "healthier" than today when they died. There was also less use of cardiotoxic medications. In addition, in the past, autopsies were performed in great numbers, and senior staff was more involved in the autopsy. Today, autopsies are only occasionally performed, usually by the most junior individuals and supervised by a staff member unable to escape the duty.

Cocaine

Cocaine is a powerfully addictive drug of abuse whose major routes of administration are sniffing (snorting), injection, and smoking (including free-base and crack cocaine). Less commonly, it is taken orally. In snorting, cocaine powder is inhaled through the nose where it is absorbed by the nasal mucosa into the bloodstream. Onset of action is 1 to 5 minutes with peak effects at 15 to 20 minutes and duration of action is 60 to 90 minutes.[6] In injection, the cocaine is introduced directly into the bloodstream. Onset of action is 10 to 60 seconds, peak effects are at 3 to 5 minutes, and duration of action is 20 to 60 minutes. Smoking involves inhaling vaporized cocaine into the lungs where it is immediately absorbed into the blood. Onset of action is 3 to 5 seconds, peak effects 1 to 3 minutes, and duration of action 5 to 15 minutes.[6] Smoking crack cocaine allows extremely high doses of cocaine to reach the brain very quickly, producing an intense and immediate high. "Crack" is the street name given to cocaine that has been processed from cocaine hydrochloride to a free base using ammonia or sodium bicarbonate (baking soda) and water and heated to remove the hydrochloride.

Physical effects of cocaine use include increased temperature, heart rate, myocardial contractility, and blood pressure. High doses of cocaine and/or prolonged use can trigger paranoia, bizarre, erratic or violent behavior, and delusions. Sudden death can occur on the first use of cocaine or unexpectedly thereafter. When individuals combine cocaine and alcohol, the liver combines cocaine and alcohol forming cocaethylene.[3] This compound intensifies cocaine's euphoric effects. It may also increase the risk of sudden death. There is no way to determine who is prone to sudden death after using cocaine. There is no specific level of the drug that causes death. The range of blood levels found in individuals dying of cocaine overdose overlaps the range found with "recreational" use.[10,11]

Cocaine activates the sympathetic nervous system both centrally and peripherally. It is a strong central nervous system stimulant that interferes with the reuptake of dopamine in the brain by strongly binding to the dopamine reuptake transporters (DATs).[3] DATs are protein structures on the membrane of presynaptic neurons that terminate dopaminergic neurotransmission by the reuptake of synaptic dopamine into the presynaptic neuron. They are the primary mechanism for the clearance of dopamine at the synapse. Therapeutic drugs such as antidepressants and antihyperactivity medications, as well as both cocaine and methamphetamine, bind to the DATs. This impairs transport of dopamine back into the nerve terminals after release, with resultant increase in dopamine at the synapse. These elevated levels of dopamine produce the high that characterizes cocaine use. Chronic cocaine abusers, in an apparent neuroadaptive measure, increase the density of DAT binding sites in the limbic striatum of the brain.[12,13] An increase in DAT function in chronic cocaine abusers is presumably due to the increased density of DAT binding sites. Interestingly and of importance was the fact that the levels of dopamine reuptake **were not elevated** in victims of excited delirium due to cocaine.[13] This possibly explains the occurrence of excited delirium in these individuals.

The central nervous system stimulation from cocaine causes increased release of norepinephrine at the peripheral synapses and epinephrine from the adrenals. Peripherally, cocaine acts to produce inhibition of norepinephrine reuptake at the synapses.[14] Thus, directly by central nervous stimulation and indirectly by blocking the reuptake of norepinephrine, cocaine causes increased concentrations of norepinephrine at the synapses between the nerve terminals and the receptors on the organs.

Intravenous injection of cocaine has demonstrated significant elevations in blood norepinephrine and epinephrine concentrations with peak levels of epinephrine at 3 minutes and norepinephrine at 12 minutes. Epinephrine levels increase more than norepinephrine.[15] The changes in epinephrine levels were correlated with changes in heart rate and systolic blood pressure with norepinephrine levels correlating with diastolic pressure and heart rate. As systolic blood pressure increases more than diastolic, it has been suggested that epinephrine has the predominant effect in cardiovascular response to cocaine.

Chronic use of cocaine is associated with cardiac injury, with increase in the size of the heart, accelerated development of atherosclerosis, and myocardial infarcts.[1–4,6] In the authors' opinion, myocardial ischemia due to the effects of markedly elevated catecholamine levels, in association with hypokalemia, is the precipitating cause of a fatal arrhythmia in individuals with excited delirium syndrome due to cocaine. The ischemia is due to the following:

1. An increase in myocardial oxygen demand resulting from increased heart rate, blood pressure, and myocardial contractility due to increased levels of epinephrine and norepinephrine at the post-ganglionic synapses of the heart. Accumulation of these catecholamines at the synapses is a result of central activation of the sympathetic nervous system due to the normal physiological response of the brain to stress (fighting, struggling) as well as due to the effects of cocaine on the brain. The activation of the sympathetic nervous system results in release of norepinephrine at the synapses and release of epinephrine and norepinephrine into the blood from the adrenals. Cocaine also acts directly at the synapses to block reuptake of the released norepinephrine.
2. A decrease in the supply of oxygen to the myocardium due to vasoconstriction of the coronary vasculature resulting from increased alpha-adrenergic stimulation; increased endothelin production and decreased nitric oxide production.
3. In some cases, accelerated atherosclerosis and thrombosis due to increased plasminogen-activator inhibitor; increased platelet activation and aggregability and increased endothelial permeability.

Increased concentrations of norepinephrine in individuals with healthy coronary arteries usually do not produce coronary artery constriction. Individuals dying of excited delirium syndrome are chronic abusers of cocaine and, thus, do not have normal vessels as a result of the continued insult from use of cocaine.[6] Thus, they are susceptible to vasoconstriction due to the effects of norepinephrine.

Methamphetamine

Methamphetamine is an addictive stimulant drug that may be taken orally, intranasally (snorting), intravenously, and by smoking. It is related chemically to amphetamine, but the central nervous system effects are greater. Immediately after smoking or injecting the drug intravenously, the user experiences an intense rush that lasts only a few minutes and is described as extremely pleasurable. Snorting or oral ingestion produces euphoria but not an intense rush. Snorting produces effects within 3 to 5 minutes; oral ingestion within 15 to 20 minutes. "Ice," the smokable form of methamphetamine, is smoked in a glass pipe like crack cocaine. The euphoria produced by methamphetamine appears similar to that produced by cocaine but the effects may last much longer. The half-life of methamphetamine ranges from 10 to 20 hours. Peak plasma levels are observed approximately 30 minutes after intravascular or intramuscular routes and 2 to 3 hours post ingestion.

Acute and chronic cardiomyopathies may occur.[16–19] They are thought to be due both to direct amphetamine toxicity on the heart and, indirectly, to amphetamine-induced hypertension, necrosis, and ischemia.

The central nervous system effects of methamphetamine are euphoria, increased wakefulness, and increased physical activity. High doses and/or chronic use results in agitation, confusion, hallucinations, paranoia, and aggressiveness. Physically, there is increased heart rate and blood pressure. Complications may include strokes, seizures, hyperthermia, secondary rhabdomyolysis, irregular heartbeat, cardiovascular collapse, and death.

Methamphetamine stimulates the sympathetic nervous system both centrally and peripherally by increasing levels of dopamine and norepinephrine. Acting on the brain, it causes the accumulation of high levels of the neurotransmitter dopamine, which stimulates brain cells.[20–22] It increases dopamine and serotonin levels by decreasing the number and activity of dopamine and serotonin transporters.[21,22] In the brain, it appears to have a neurotoxic effect, damaging axons and axon terminals.[21,22]

In the authors' opinion, myocardial ischemia due to the action of catecholamines, in association with hypokalemia, is the precipitating cause of death in individuals with excited delirium syndrome due to methamphetamine. The ischemia is due to the following:

1. An increase in myocardial oxygen demand resulting from the increased heart rate, blood pressure, and myocardial contractility due to increased levels of epinephrine and norepinephrine at the postganglionic synapses of the heart. Accumulation of these catecholamines at the synapses is due to central activation of the sympathetic nervous system by stress and the action of methamphetamine on the brain, with resultant release of norepinephrine

at the synapses and release of epinephrine and norepinephrine into the blood from the adrenals. Methamphetamine also acts directly at the synapses by causing increased release of norepinephrine by the axon.

2. A decrease in the supply of oxygen to the myocardium due to vasoconstriction of the coronary vasculature. Increased concentrations of norepinephrine in individuals with healthy coronary arteries usually do not produce coronary artery constriction. Individuals dying of excited delirium syndrome are chronic abusers of methamphetamine and thus do not have normal vessels as a result of the continued insult from use of methamphetamine. Thus, they are susceptible to vasoconstriction due to the effects of norepinephrine.

Unlike cocaine, one can have flashbacks from use of methamphetamine. Thus, one can discontinue use of methamphetamine but have an episode of paranoid delirium months later.[23,24]

PCP[25]

PCP (phencyclidine) or *angel dust* was developed in the 1950s as an intravenous anesthetic.[25] It is a noncompetitive antagonist of the N-methyl-D-aspartate (NMDA)/glutamate receptors. Use in humans was discontinued in 1965 because patients often became agitated, delusional, and irrational while recovering from its anesthetic effects. It is snorted, smoked, or ingested. For smoking, PCP is often applied to a leafy material such as marijuana. The physical effects of its use include a rise in blood pressure and pulse rate, flushing, profuse sweating, numbness of the extremities, and loss of muscular coordination. Psychological effects mimic the symptoms of schizophrenia: delusions, hallucinations, paranoia, disordered thinking, and violent behavior.

PCP was used in the past to produce experimental models of schizophrenia in humans. Repeated use of PCP may produce persistent symptoms of schizophrenia: psychosis, hallucinations, delusions, thought disorders, cognitive dysfunction, and flattened affect.

Symptoms can persist up to a year after stopping PCP use. PCP has sedative effects, and interacts with other central nervous system depressants, e.g., alcohol, with resultant coma or death.

PCP stimulates the autonomic system centrally. In the authors' opinion, myocardial ischemia, in association with catecholamine toxicity is the precipitating cause of death in individuals with excited delirium syndrome due to PCP.

Alcohol

Sudden death during a struggle in an individual with a history of alcohol abuse and in whom only alcohol may be present occasionally occurs. Alcohol is a recognized cause of a variety of atrial and ventricular arrhythmias.[26,27] In addition, chronic alcohol abusers have been found to have a prolonged QT interval.[28,29] In one study, 46.8% of patients in alcohol withdrawl showed prolonged QTc intervals.[29] The intervals became normal with remission of symptoms. Alcohol causes a hyperadrenergic state. Alcoholism has been associated with increased levels of norepinephrine.[30] All these predispositions to arrhythmias can be aggravated by catecholamines released during a violent struggle. Thus, if the heart is predisposed to fatal arrhythmias by the action of alcohol, then under conditions such as a violent struggle, the released catecholamines can produce a fatal arrhythmia.

PSYCHOTROPIC DRUGS AND SUDDEN DEATH

Antidepressants

Antidepressants fall into two general categories: the tricyclic antidepressants (TCAs) and the selective serotonin reuptake inhibitors (SSRIs).[31,32] The TCAs block reuptake of two neurotransmitters norepinephrine and serotonin, with greater activity in blocking the reuptake of norepinephrine. Blocking reuptake of serotonin and norepinephrine increases the concentration of these drugs at the synapse with resultant relief in depression. The TCAs are so named because most of them have a chemical structure that includes three rings. The TCAs were the first medications to come into widespread use for the treatment of depression.

There are two broad chemical classes of TCAs. The tertiary amines (amitriptyline, imipramine, and doxepin) have proportionally more effect in increasing serotonin levels than norepinephrine and produce more sedation and orthostatic hypotension. The secondary amines (nortriptyline, desipramine) tend more toward increasing norepinephrine levels and hence toward overstimulation.

Arrhythmias and *heart block* occasionally follow the use of TCAs, particularly amitriptyline, and may be a factor in the sudden death of patients with cardiac disease.[33,34] **Imipramine** and **amitriptyline** have more marked cardiac side effects than other TCAs.[35] Reports have linked TCAs with *torsade de pointes* (a ventricular tachycardia that may progress to ventricular fibrillation).[36] TCA-induced cardiotoxicity is due to their ability to cause prolonged depolarization, manifested by widened QRS complexes.[34–36] TCAs act on both sodium (fast) channels but also on delayed rectifier potassium (I_{Kr}) channels. Blockade of the potassium channels rather than their action on sodium channels more likely explains the ability of TCAs to prolong the QT interval and provoke torsade de pointes.[36]

The TCAs have been largely replaced by the SSRIs and are now considered "older" or "first generation" antidepressants. The SSRIs block reuptake of serotonin by blocking the presynaptic serotonin transporter receptor, thus reducing the amount of dopamine.[31] The primary uses for the SSRIs include unipolar and bipolar major depression and all of the anxiety disorders. In contrast to TCAs, SSRIs are more potent inhibitors of serotonin reuptake, and have less of an effect on other receptors. The available SSRIs differ from each other in that some affect not only the serotonin presynaptic transporter but also to a lesser degree the norepinephrine and/or the dopamine transporters. Fluoxetine and paroxetine have a greater effect on the norepinephrine transporters than the other SSRIs. SSRIs commonly available in the United States are citalopram (Celexa), fluoxetine (Prozac), fluvoxamine (Luvox), paroxetine (Paxil), and sertraline (Zoloft).

Antidepressants are encountered in association with excited delirium syndrome when the individual has bipolar disease. These medications are used to treat the depressive cycle of the bipolar disease. Antidepressants, however, can accelerate cycling and induce mania in the formerly depressed individual. Because some of the TCAs have the potential to produce an arrhythmia, they may be a contributory factor in the death of bipolar individuals in the manic phase.

Antipsychotics

Currently available antipsychotic medications alleviate the symptoms of schizophrenia by decreasing dopamine-mediated neurotransmission.[37] The first antipsychotic drug used to treat schizophrenia was chlorpromazine. It and all other first-generation antipsychotic drugs produce an immediate blockade of dopamine D2 receptors.[37] While subsequently developed first-generation drugs were more potent dopamine antagonists than chlorpromazine, they were found to be no more effective. Examples of first-generation antipsychotics are chlorpromazine, haloperidol, and thioridazine. The first-generation drugs had significant side effects. One of these was neuroleptic malignant syndrome in which a patient's temperature exceeds 104°F with resultant brain death. This is apparently due to polymorphism in a D2 dopamine receptor.[37]

First-generation antipsychotics have been replaced to a significant degree by second-generation or atypical antipsychotic drugs. The atypical antipsychotic agents are different chemically from the older drugs used to treat psychosis. They are considered *atypical* because they have different side effects from the conventional antipsychotic agents. The drugs in this group are clozapine, risperidone, olanzapine, quetiapine, ziprasidone, and aripiprazole. They are also D2 dopamine receptor antagonists, although this is not the sole therapeutic mechanism.[37]

The QT interval demonstrated by electrocardiography measures depolarization and repolarization of the heart. Since the QT interval depends on heart rate, the QT is usually corrected for heart rate and is often stated as the QTc. The QT interval visualized on the electrocardiogram reflects not only the ventricular conduction time but also the ventricular action potential at the cellular level. The upstroke of the QT interval on the electrocardiogram represents depolarization due to inward flux of Na^+ ions into the cells with repolarization due primarily to outward flux of K^+.[33,34] Prolongation of the QT interval is associated with the ventricular tachyarrhythmia torsade de pointes and sudden death.[34,38] Just because a drug produces a prolonged QT interval, however, does not mean that it produces torsade de pointes and sudden death.

Psychotropic drugs, e.g. antipsychotics, neuroleptics, antidepressants, stimulants, and antianxiety agents may cause cardiac arrhythmias and sudden death.[33–45] The TCAs, e.g., imipramine and amitriptyline, phenothiazine-derivatived antipsychotics such as thioridazine, as well as some of the newer atypical antipsychotics may cause QT prolongation and sudden cardiac death. The risk of cardiac arrhythmia from these medications at therapeutic levels probably involves individual sensitivity, i.e., a subpopulation of vulnerable individuals. Arrhythmia due to TCAs is more common in individuals with conduction abnormalities and/or heart disease.[34] The advantage of the SSRIs over TCAs is that SSRIs have a wider range of safety as they are rarely associated with cardiotoxic effects and prolongation of the QT interval.[34]

Some antipsychotic drugs, especially the phenothiazines, are associated with repolarization anomalies including prolongation of the QT interval.[33,34,38–45] Most of these are first-generation antipsychotics. Thioridazine and droperidol are associated with prolongation of the QT even at therapeutic doses. With the exception of sertindole and ziprasidone, the atypical antipsychotics have not been proved to be associated with QT prolongation or sudden death at therapeutic levels. The association between prolonged QT and sudden cardiac death is greater for some antipsychotics (thioridazine and droperidol) than for TCAs.[33,34] Haloperidol, which is widely used, has also been associated with prolongation of the QT interval and sudden death.[33,39]

Antipsychotics, both first-generation and atypical, are used not only in the treatment of schizophrenia but also bipolar disease. Thus, haloperidol and chlorpromazine are used for managing extreme agitation. Unfortunately, many of these medications, including the two cited, are associated with prolongation of the QT interval and, thus, sudden death.[33]

Haloperidol is routinely given to individuals in delirium. An individual in excited delirium who gets to an emergency room, in all probability, will be given haloperidol. Only quite recently has it been realized that haloperidol can produce torsade de pointes and QT prolongation. In most instances, this involves high doses given intravenously,[39] but this is not always the case: especially in the presence of factors increasing susceptibility QT, torsade de pointes, and QT prolongation can occur in association with normal doses.[33] Factors increasing susceptibility are hypokalemia, hypocalcemia, hypothyroidism, and hypomagnesemia.

Control of the duration of the action potential of ventricular myocytes is based on an equilibrium between inward and outward currents of ions across the cell membrane. The longer action potential demonstrated by QT prolongation results from an imbalance in the flow.[33,34,38,40–45] Many TCAs and neuroleptics can block outward movement of K^+ and thus repolarization. These drugs include imipramine, amitriptyline, trazodone, maprotiline, and mianserine. This results in a greater risk of an arrhythmia. Some psychotropic drugs (chlorpromazine, haloperidol, and imipramine) inhibit inward ionic currents. especially Na^+ and Ca^{2+}.

Increased sympathetic activity can be a factor in development of a ventricular arrhythmia in individuals with coronary artery disease. It has been speculated that in schizophrenia, where there is known to be increased norepinephrine levels, there may be increased risk of an arrhythmia due to increases in sympathetic activity resulting from blockade of norepinephrine reuptake by some psychotropic drugs, e.g., desipramine. In contrast, psychotropic drugs that increase serotonin levels in the brain by blockade of serotonin reuptake, e.g., clomipramine, produce a reduction of sympathetic activity increasing the threshold for an arrhythmia.

Diphenhydramine

Diphenhydramine (DPH) is a common ingredient in over-the-counter cold and allergy medications. It is also used as a mild sleep-inducing agent by both the public and physicians. It is generally considered a relatively harmless drug with deaths due to it being rare.[46] Diphenhydramine blocks muscarine receptors in the body causing an anticholinergic effect. As diphenhydramine has both antihistamine and anticholinergic properties, in high doses it can have both central nervous system effects and cardiac toxicity. One presentation of diphenhydramine toxicity is excited delirium.[47,48] Diphenhydramine is potentially cardiotoxic by virtue of its ability to prolong cardiac repolarization by blocking fast sodium channels and, more importantly, HERG potassium channels.[49–51] In this it is similar to

TCAs. Overdose with diphenhydramine produces prolongation of the QRS interval and tachycardia. There is one reported case of torsade de pointes attributable to diphenhydramine.[51]

MISCELLANEOUS DRUGS

A number of other drugs besides the drugs previously cited in this chapter can cause delirium and acute psychosis. These include marijuana, albuterol, promethazine, and epileptic medications.[52–56] Herbal remedies such as St. John's wort have also been linked to episodes of mania.[57]

REFERENCES

1. Karch, S.B., Green, G.S. et al. Myocardial hypertrophy and coronary artery disease in male cocaine users. *J. Forensic Sci.* 40(4):591–595, 1995.
2. Wiener, R.S., Lockhart, J.T., and Schwartz, R.G. Dilated cardiomyopathy and cocaine abuse: report of two cases. *Am. J. Med.* 81:699–701, 1986.
3. Karch, S.B. *Karch's Pathology of Drug Abuse,* 3rd. ed. CRC Press, Boca Raton, FL, 2002.
4. Silver, M.D., Gotlieb, A.I., and Schoen, F.J. *Cardiovascular Pathology.* Churchill Livingstone, Philadelphia, 2001.
5. Spitito, P., Bellone, P. et al. Magnitude of left ventricular hypertrophy and risk of sudden death in hypertrophic cardiomyopathy. *N. Engl. J. Med.* 342(24):1778–1785, 2000.
6. Lange, R.A. and Hillus, L.D. Cardiovascular complications of cocaine use (medical progress). *N. Engl. J. Med.* 345(5):351–358, 2001.
7. Sunderman, W.F. and Borner, F. *Normal Values in Clinical Medicine.* W.B. Saunders, Philadelphia, 1949.
8. Zeek, P.M. *Arch. Pathol.* 34:820–832, 1942.
9. Kitzman, D.W., Scholz, D.G., Hagen, P.T., Ilstrup. D.M., and Edwards, W.D. Age-related changes in normal human hearts during the first 10 decades of life. Part II (maturity): a quantitative anatomic study of 765 specimens from subjects 20 to 99 years old. *Mayo Clin. Proc.* 63(2):137–146, 1988.
10. Karch, S.B. and Stephens, B.G. Acute excited states and sudden death; acute excited states are not caused by high blood concentrations of cocaine. *Br. Med. J.* 316(7138):1171, 1998.
11. Karch, S.B., Stephens, B., and Ho, C.H. Relating cocaine blood concentrations to toxicity — an autopsy study of 99 cases. *J. Forensic Sci.* 43(1):41–45, 1998.
12. Staley, J.K., Hearn, W.L., Ruttenber, A.J., Wetli, C.V., and Mash, D.C. High affinity cocaine recognition sites on the dopamine transporter are elevated in fatal cocaine overdose victims. *J. Pharmacol. Exp. Ther.* 271:1678–1685, 1994.
13. Mash, D.C., Pablo, J., Ouyang, Q., Hearn, W.L., and Izenwasser, S. Dopamine transport function is elevated in cocaine users. *J. Neurochem.* 81:292–300, 2002.
14. Billman, G.E. Cocaine: a review of the toxic actions on cardiac function. *Crit. Rev. Toxicol.* 25:113, 1995.
15. Sofuoglu, M., Nelson, D., Babb, D.A., and Hatsukami, D.K. Intravenous cocaine increases plasma epinephrine and norepinephrine in humans. *Pharm. Biochem. Behav.* 68:455–459, 2001.

16. Karch, S.B., Stephens, B.G., and Ho, C.H. Methamphetamine related deaths in San Francisco: demographic, pathologic and toxicologic profiles. *J. Forensic Sci.* 44(2):359–368, 1999.

17. Logan, B.K., Fligner, C.L., and Haddix, T. Cause and manner of death in fatalities involving methamphetamine. *J. Forensic Sci.* 43(1):28–34, 1998.

18. Hong, R., Matsuyama, E., and Nur, K. Cardiomyopathy associated with the smoking of crystal methamphetamine. *J. Am. Med. Assoc.* 265(9):1152–1154, 1991.

19. Yu, Q., Larson, D.F., and Watson, R.R. Heart disease, methamphetamine and AIDS. *Life Sci.* 73(2):129–140, 2003.

20. Hanson, G.R., Rau, K.S., and Fleckenstein, A.E. The methamphetamine experience: a NIDA partnership. *Neuropharmacology* 47(Suppl. 1):92–100, 2004.

21. Fleckenstein, A.E., Gibb, J.W., and Hanson, G.R. Differential effects of stimulants on monoaminergic transporters: pharmacological consequences and implications for neurotoxicity. *Eur. J. Pharmacol.* 406(1):1–13, 2000.

22. McCann, U.D. and Ricaurte, G.A. Amphetamine neurotoxicity: accomplishments and remaining challenges. *Neurosci. Biobehav. Rev.* 27(8):821–826, 2004.

23. Yui, K., Jshiguro, T., Goto, K., and Ikemoto, S. Precipitating factors in spontaneous recurrence of methamphetamine psychosis. *Psychopharmacology* 134:303–308, 1997.

24. Yui, K., Goto, K., Ikemoto, S., and Ishiguro, T. Stress induced spontaneous recurrence of methamphetamine psychosis: the relation between stressful experiences and sensitivity to stress. *Drug Alcohol Dependence* 58(1–2):67–75, 2000.

25. Jentsch, J.D. and Roth, R.H. The neuropsychopharmacology of phencyclidine: from NMDA receptor hypofunction to the dopamine hypothesis of schizophrenia. *Neuropsychopharmacology* 20(3):201–225, 1999.

26. Singer, K. and Lundberg, W.B. Ventricular arrythmias associated with the ingestion of alcohol. *Ann. Intern. Med.* 77:247–248, 1972.

27. Ettinger, P.O., Wu, C.F., De La Cruz, C., Jr., Weisse, A.B., Ahmed, S.S., and Regan, T.J. Arrhythmias and the "Holiday Heart": alcohol-associated cardiac rhythm disorders. *Am. Heart J.* 95(5):555–562, 1978.

28. Day, C.P., James, O.F., Butler, T.J., and Campbell, R.W. QT prolongation and sudden cardiac death in patients with alcoholic liver disease. *Lancet* 341(8858):1423–1428, 1993.

29. Bernardi, M., Calandra, S., Colantoni, A., Trevisani, F., Raimondo, M.L., Sica, G., Schepis, F., Mandini, M., Simoni, P., Contin, M., and Raimondo, G. Q-T interval prolongation in cirrhosis: prevalence, relationship with severity, and etiology of the disease and possible pathogenetic factors. *Hepatology* 27(1):28–34, 1998.

30. Newsome, H.H., Jr. Ethanol modulation of plasma norepinephrine response to trauma and hemorrhage. *J. Trauma-Injury Infection Crit. Care* 28(1):1–9, 1988.

31. Zohar, J. and Westenberg, H.G. Anxiety disorders: a review of tricyclic antidepressants and selective serotonin reuptake inhibitors. *Acta Psychiatr. Scand. Suppl.* 403:39–49, 2000.

32. Peretti, S., Judge, R., and Hindmarch, I. Safety and tolerability considerations: tricyclic antidepressants vs. selective serotonin reuptake inhibitors. *Acta Psychiatr. Scand. Suppl.* 403:17–25, 2000.

33. Glassman, A.H. and Bigger, J.T., Jr. Antipsychotic drugs: prolonged QTc interval, torsade de pointes, and sudden death. *Am. J. Psychiatr.* 158(11):1774–1782, 2001.

34. Witchel, H.J., Hancox, J.C., and Nutt, D.J. Psychotropic drugs, cardiac arrhythmia, and sudden death. *J. Clin. Psychopharmacol.* 23(1):58–77, 2003.

35. Teschemacher, A.G., Seward, E.P., Hancox, J.C., and Witchel, H.J. Inhibition of the current of heterologously expressed HERG potassium channels by imipramine and amitriptyline. *Br. J. Pharmacol.* 128(2):479–485, 1999.

36. Vieweg, W.V. and Wood, M.A. Tricyclic antidepressants, QT interval prolongation, and torsade de pointes. *Psychosomatics* 45(5):371–377, 2004.

37. Freedman, R. Drug therapy: schizophrenia (review article). *N. Engl. J. Med.* 349(18):1738–1749, 2003.

38. Roden, D.M. Drug-induced prolongation of the QT interval. *N. Engl. J. Med.* 350(10):1013–1022, 2004.

39. Hassaballa, H.A. and Balk, R.A. Torsade de pointes associated with the administration of intravenous haloperidol: a review of the literature and practical guidelines for use. *Expert Opin. Drug Saf.* 2(6):543–7, 2003.

40. Fayek, M., Kingsbury, S.J., Zada, J., and Simpson, G.M. Psychopharmacology: cardiac effects of antipsychotic medications. *Psychiatr. Serv.* 52:607–609, 2001.

41. Haddad, P.M. and Anderson, I.M. Antipsychotic-related QTc prolongation, torsade de pointes and sudden death. *Drugs* 62(11):1649–1671, 2002.

42. Zareba, W. and Lin, D.A. Antipsychotic drugs and QT interval prolongation. *Psychiatr. Q.* 74(3):291–306, 2003.

43. Kongsamut, S., Kang, J., Chen, X.L., Roehr, J., and Rampe, D. A comparison of the receptor binding and HERG channel affinities for a series of antipsychotic drugs. *Eur. J. Pharmacol.* 450(1):37–41, 2002.

44. Straus, S.M., Bleumink, G.S., Dieleman, J.P., van der Lei, J., 't Jong, G.W., Kingma, J.H., Sturkenboom, M.C., and Stricker, B.H. Antipsychotics and the risk of sudden cardiac death. *Arch. Intern. Med.* 164(12):1293–1297, 2004.

45. Herxheimer, A. Arrhythmias and sudden death in patients taking antipsychotic drugs. *Br. Med. J.* 325:1253–1254, 2002.

46. Koppel, C., Ibe, K., and Tenczer, J. Clinical symptomatology of diphenhydramine overdose: an evaluation of 136 cases in 1982 to 1985. *J. Toxicol. Clin. Toxicol.* 25(1–2):53–70, 1987.

47. Sexton, J.D. and Pronchik, D.J. Diphenhydramine-induced psychosis with therapeutic doses. *Am. J. Emerg. Med.* 15(5):548–9, 1997.

48. Serio, R.N. Acute delirium associated with combined diphenhydramine and linezolid use. *Ann. Pharmacother.* 38(1):62–65, 2004.

49. Kuo, C.C., Huang, R.C., and Lou, B.S. Inhibition of Na(+) current by diphenhydramine and other diphenyl compounds: molecular determinants of selective binding to the inactivated channels. *Mol. Pharmacol.* 57(1):135–143, 2000.

50. Sharma, A.N., Hexdall, A.H., Chang, E.K., Nelson, L.S., and Hoffman, R.S. Diphenhydramine-induced wide complex dysrhythmia responds to treatment with sodium bicarbonate. *Am. J. Emerg. Med.* 21(3):212–215, 2003.

51. Joshi, A.K., Sljapic, T., Borghei, H., and Kowey, P.R. Case of polymorphic ventricular tachycardia in diphenhydramine poisoning. *J. Cardiovasc. Electrophysiol.* 15(5):591–593, 2004.

52. Iversen, L. Cannabis and the brain. *Brain* 126(Pt 6):1252–1270, 2003.

53. Kalant, H. Adverse effects of cannabis on health: an update of the literature since 1996. *Progress in Neuro-Psychopharmacology & Biological Psychiatry* 28(5):849–863, 2004.

54. Martin, W., Unutzer, J., Szuba, M.P. Exacerbation of psychosis associated with inhaled albuterol. *Journal of Clinical Psychopharmacology* 15(6):446–447, 1995.
55. Timnak, C. and Gleason, O. Promethazine-induced psychosis in a 16-year-old girl. *Psychosomatics* 45(1):89–90, 2004.
56. Matsuura, M. Epileptic psychoses and anticonvulsant drug treatment. *Journal of Neurology, Neurosurgery & Psychiatry* 67(2):231–233, 1999.
57. Stevinson, C. and Ernst E. Can St. John's wort trigger psychoses? *International Journal of Clinical Pharmacology & Therapeutics* 42(9):473–480, 2004.

ADDITIONAL REFERENCES

Pestaner, J.P. and Southall, P.E., Sudden death during arrest and phencyclidine intoxication. *Am. J. Forensic Pathol.* 24:119–122, 2003.

6

SYNTHESIS OF PHYSIOLOGICAL REACTIONS TO STRESS, NATURAL DISEASE, DRUGS OF ABUSE, AND MEDICATIONS IN CASES OF EXCITED DELIRIUM

Excited delirium syndrome involves the sudden death of an individual, during or following an episode of excited delirium, in which an autopsy fails to reveal evidence of sufficient trauma or natural disease to explain the death. In virtually all such cases, the episode of excited delirium is terminated by a struggle with police or medical personnel, and the use of physical restraint. Typically, within a few to several minutes following cessation of the struggle, the individual is noted to be in cardiopulmonary arrest. Attempts at resuscitation are usually unsuccessful. Virtually all individuals dying of excited delirium syndrome are on illegal stimulants, e.g., cocaine, or medications that either duplicate the effects of cocaine on the nervous system or prolong the QT interval. In some cases, underlying natural disease contributes to the death. Some individuals may also have a genetic predisposition due to polymorphism of cardiac receptor sites.

For many years, it was believed that death in excited delirium syndrome was due to positional or restraint asphyxia.[1-5] The problem with this hypothesis is that experiments by Chan et al. have essentially disproved this hypothesis.[6] There is no scientific evidence that restraint results in hypoxia. Proponents of this discredited theory now postulate that the asphyxia is due to compression of the chest by police or medical personnel. Not only is this hypothesis not supported by scientific studies, but it is actually contradicted by experiments by Chan et al.[7] In addition, cardiopulmonary arrest in cases of excited delirium syndrome typically occurs after the struggle has ceased, when no pressure is being applied to the chest. In the 22 cases presented in this book in Chapter 8, in only one instance did the arrest occur while pressure was being applied to the chest. In the other cases, the individuals were restrained, and had stopped struggling before cardiac arrest occurred.

Can positional asphyxia cause or contribute to a death after restraint? Yes, but this almost always involves circumstances such as massive obesity and/or unusual positioning of the individual, e.g., being placed in the back of a police vehicle wedged between the front- and backseat with the abdomen over the transmission hump.

Why then do some individuals in excited delirium die? They do not die of restraint or positional asphyxia as, in virtually all cases, asphyxia plays no role in the deaths. The cause of death in these cases is multifactorial. It is due primarily to a hyperadrenergic state combined with the actions of stimulants and/or medications affecting the QT interval and/or natural disease and/or genetic polymorphism.

Whenever one engages in any strenuous physical activity, whether it is a struggle or exercise, there is activation of the sympathetic nervous system with release of catecholamines (norepinephrine and epinephrine). These cause the heart to beat harder and faster and to raise the blood pressure. At the same time, there may be constriction of the coronary arteries with reduction of blood flow, and thus oxygen, to the myocardium.[8] This constriction occurs if there is any damage or disease present in the coronary arteries such as is seen in chronic cocaine abuse.[9] Peak levels of catecholamines are reached not during the physical activity but in the 2 to 5 minutes after cessation of the activity and may reach ten times base levels.[10] This is Dimsdale et al.'s "period of peril" when the heart is most sensitive to development of fatal arrhythmias.

During the physical activity, blood potassium also increases.[11] Elevated levels of catecholamines in the blood neutralize the arrythmogenic potential of the elevated blood potassium.[12,13] During the "period of peril," the blood potassium drops dramatically, at times to hypokalemic levels. Hypokalemia, like hyperkalemia, is arrythmogenic, but its effects are not protected by elevated blood catecholamine levels. Hypokalemia predisposes one to prolongation of the QT interval, development of torsade de pointes, and sudden cardiac death.[14] Thus, anyone engaging in a struggle or strenuous physical activity, after cessation of the struggle, enters a "period of peril" characterized by peak levels of catecholamines and dramatically falling levels of potassium. While the usual result of these physiological changes is uneventful with a complete return to normal health, in some individuals, especially those in excited delirium (ED), death can result. Even in individuals in ED, this is a rare outcome. In some individuals, the effects of norepinephrine may be magnified by a genetic predisposition due to polymorphism of cardiac receptor sites.[15,16]

Stimulants such as cocaine and methamphetamine have both direct and indirect central nervous system and peripheral effects.[9,17–19] Centrally, the drugs directly activate the sympathetic nervous system by increasing levels of dopamine and norepinephrine in the brain. This stimulation results in release of increased quantities of norepinephrine at the synapses between the nerves and the receptor organs, and norepinephrine and epinephrine from the adrenals. Chronic stimulation predisposes individuals to a state of excited delirium. The agitation and struggling resulting from excited delirium will result in additional stimulation of the sympathetic nervous system, independently of the direct action on the brain by the drugs themselves.

Peripherally, these stimulants cause increased release of norepinephrine from the presynaptic neurons and/or decreases in reuptake of norepinephrine. Both of these actions cause an increase in the concentration of norepinephrine at the synapse and increase stimulation of the postsynaptic receptors. The result of both the central nervous system and peripheral effects of these drugs is a hyperadrenergic state from the drugs superimposed on the hyperadrenergic state from the struggle. The heart then beats faster and harder and the coronary arteries, which are not normal because of chronic use of stimulants, contract, decreasing the oxygenation of the myocardium and predisposing the heart to a fatal cardiac arrhythmia.

Medications also can contribute to death in cases of excited delirium. The tricyclic antidepressants (TCAs) block reuptake of two neurotransmitters, norepinephrine and serotonin, with greater activity in blocking the reuptake of norepinephrine.[20] *Arrhythmias* and *heart block* occasionally follow the use of TCAs, particularly amitriptyline, and may be a factor in the sudden death of patients with cardiac disease. TCA-induced cardiotoxicity is due to the ability of the drugs to cause prolonged depolarization, manifested by widened QRS complexes. TCAs block both the sodium (fast) channels and the rectifier potassium (I_{Kr}) channels. Blockade of the potassium channels rather than their action on sodium channels more likely explains the capability of TCAs to prolong the QT interval and provoke torsade de pointes.[21,22]

Antipsychotic medications alleviate the symptoms of schizophrenia by decreasing dopamine-mediated neurotransmission. Some antipsychotic drugs, especially the phenothiazines, are associated with repolarization anomalies, including prolongation of the QT interval.[23–29] Chronic alcohol abuse is also associated with prolongation of the QT interval.[30,31]

A substantial degree of polymorphism or variation occurs in genes in the general population.[15] The combination of two receptor variants in the heart, resulting in an increase in norepinephrine release and enhanced β_1 receptor function at the cardiac myocyte, appears to act synergistically to increase the levels of norepinephrine and its effect on heart cells.[16] Thus, we have a hyperadrenergic state due to this genetic variation. The presence of polymorphic α_2 and β_1 receptors may explain why some individuals die following the physical stress of excited delirium syndrome while the bulk of the population does not.

There is also the effect of underlying natural disease, especially cardiac disease. Death from excited delirium syndrome may occur in association with natural disease. The disease may be of a significant degree but not so advanced as to cause death by itself under ordinary circumstances. Chronic abuse of stimulants can initiate and accelerate "natural disease." Thus, cocaine causes enlargement of the heart and accelerated coronary atherosclerosis.[9,17,32,33]

In conclusion, it is the opinion of the authors that death in the excited delirium syndrome results from a fatal cardiac arrhythmia due to a **hyperadrenergic state** caused by:

1. The excited delirium, which in itself triggers release of catecholamine
2. Additional release of catecholamines due to the struggle
3. A rapid and steep drop in blood potassium concentrations following cessation of the struggle in association with increasing levels of catecholamines

The hyperadrenergic state is almost invariably aggravated by the effects of:

1. Illegal stimulants. which directly and indirectly cause increased levels of catecholamines
2. Medications that have either the same actions as the stimulants in causing increased concentrations of catecholamines and/or cause prolongation of the QT interval
3. The presence of natural disease of a degree insufficient in itself to cause death but when in combination with a hyperadrenergic state can do so

In some instances, there may be a greater potential to develop a hyperadrenergic state due to genetic polymorphism in the heart. In occasional cases, the cause of death in excited delirium syndrome will be positional or traumatic asphyxia.

REFERENCES

1. Reay, D.T., Fligner, C.L., Stilwell, A.D., and Arnold, J. Positional asphyxia during law enforcement transport. *Am. J. Forensic Med. Pathol.* 13(2):90–97, 1992.
2. O'Halloran, R.L. and Lewman, L.V. Restraint asphyxiation in excited delirium. *Am. J. Forensic Med. Pathol.* 14(4):289–295, 1993.
3. O'Halloran, R.L. and Frank, J.G. Asphyxial death during prone restraint position revisited: a report of 21 cases. *Am. J. Forensic Med. Pathol.* 21(1):39–52, 2000.
4. Stratton, S.J., Rogers, C., and Green, K. Sudden death in individuals in hobble restraints during paramedic transport. *Ann. Emerg. Med.* 25(5):710–712, 1995.
5. Pollanen, M., Chiasson, D.A., and Cairns, J.T. Unexpected death related to restraint for excited delirium: a retrospective study of deaths in police custody and in the community. *Can. Med. Assoc. J.* 158(12):1603–1607, 1998.
6. Chan, T.C., Vilke, G.N., Neuman, T., and Clausen, J.L. Restraint position and positional asphyxia. *Ann. Emerg. Med.* 30:578–586, 1997.
7. Chan, T.C., Neuman, T., Clausen, J., Eisele, J., and Vilke, G.M. Weight force during prone restraint and respiratory function. *Am. J. Forensic Med. Pathol.* 25(3):185–189, 2004.
8. Heusch, G., Baumgart, D., Camici, P. et al. [alpha]-Adrenergic coronary vasoconstriction and myocardial ischemia in humans. *Circulation* 101(6):689–694, 2000.
9. Lange, R.A. and Hillis, L.D. Cardiovascular complications of cocaine use. *N. Engl. J. Med.* 345(5):351–358, 2001.
10. Dimsdale, J.E., Hartley, G.T., Guiney, T., Ruskin, J.N., and Greenblatt, D. Post-exercise peril: plasma catecholamines and exercise. *J. Am. Med. Assoc.* 251:630–632, 1984.
11. Young, D.B., Srivastava, T.N., Fitzovich, D.E., Kivlighn, S.D., and Hamaguchi, M. Potassium and catecholamine concentrations in the immediate post exercise period. *Am. J. Med. Sci.* 304:150–153, 1992.
12. Paterson, D.J., Rogers, J., Powell, T., and Brown, H.F. Effect of catecholamines on the ventricular myocyte action potential in raised extracellular potassium. *Acta Physiol. Scand.* 148:177–186, 1993.
13. Leitch, S.P. and Paterson, D.J. Interactive effects of K^+, acidosis, and catecholamines on isolated rabbit heart: implications for exercise. *J. Appl. Physiol.* 77(3):1164–1171, 1994.
14. Gennar, F.J. Current concepts: hypokalemia (review article). *N. Engl. J. Med.* 339(7):451–458, 1998.
15. Hajjar, R.J. and MacRae, C.A. Editorial: Adrenergic-receptor polymorphism and heart failure. *N. Engl. J. Med.* 347(15):1196–1198, 2002.
16. Small, K.M., Wagoner, L.E., Levin, A.M., Kardia, S.L.R., and Liggett, S.B. Synergistic polymorphisms of B_1 and alpha $_{2c}$ adrenergic receptors and the risk of congestive heart failure. *N. Engl. J. Med.* 347(15):1135–1142, 2002.
17. Karch, S.B. *Karch's Pathology of Drug Abuse,* 3rd ed. CRC Press, Boca Raton, FL, 2002.
18. Sofuoglu, M., Nelson, D., Babb, D.A., and Hatsukami, D.K. Intravenous cocaine increases plasma epinephrine and norepinephrine in humans. *Pharm. Biochem. Behav.* 68:445–459, 2001.

19. Vongpatanasin, W., Mansour, Y., Chavoshan, B., et al. Cocaine stimulates the human cardiovascular system via a central mechanism of action. *Circulation* 100:497–502, 1999.

20. Owens, M.J. Molecular and cellular mechanisms of antidepressant drugs. *Depression Anxiety* 4(4):153–159, 1996–1997.

21. Teschemacher, A.G., Seward, E.P., Hancox, J.C., and Witchel, H.J. Inhibition of the current of heterologously expressed HERG potassium channels by imipramine and amitriptyline. *Br. J. Pharmacol.* 128(2):479–485, 1999.

22. Vieweg, W.V. and Wood, M.A. Tricyclic antidepressants, QT interval prolongation, and torsade de pointes. *Psychosomatics* 45(5):371–377, 2004.

23. Straus, S.M., Bleumink, G.S., Dieleman, J.P., van der Lei, J., 't Jong, G.W., Kingma, J.H., Sturkenboom, M.C., and Stricker, B.H. Antipsychotics and the risk of sudden cardiac death. *Arch. Intern. Med.* 164(12):1293–1297, 2004.

24. Haddad, P.M. and Anderson, I.M. Antipsychotic-related QTc prolongation, torsade de pointes and sudden death. *Drugs* 62(11):1649–1671, 2002.

25. Witchel, H.J., Hancox, J.C., and Nutt, D.J. Psychotropic drugs, cardiac arrhythmia, and sudden death. *J. Clin. Psychopharmacol.* 23(1):58–77, 2003.

26. Glassman, A.H. and Bigger, J.T., Jr. Antipsychotic drugs: prolonged QTc interval, torsade de pointes, and sudden death. *Am. J. Psychiatr.* 158(11):1774–1782, 2001.

27. Fayek, M., Kingsbury, S.J., Zada, J., and Simpson, G.M. Psychopharmacology: cardiac effects of antipsychotic medications. *Psychiatr. Serv.* 52:607–609, 2001.

28. Zareba, W. and Lin, D.A. Antipsychotic drugs and QT interval prolongation. *Psychiatr. Q.* 74(3):291–306, 2003.

29. Herxheimer, A. Arrhythmias and sudden death in patients taking antipsychotic drugs. *Br. Med. J.* 325:1253–1254, 2002.

30. Day, C.P., James, O.F., Butler, T.J., and Campbell, R.W. QT prolongation and sudden cardiac death in patients with alcoholic liver disease. *Lancet* 341(8858):1423–1428, 1993.

31. Bernardi, M., Calandra, S., Colantoni, A., Trevisani, F., Raimondo, M.L., Sica, G., Schepis, F., Mandini, M., Simoni, P., Contin, M., and Raimondo G. Q-T interval prolongation in cirrhosis: prevalence, relationship with severity, and etiology of the disease and possible pathogenetic factors. *Hepatology* 27(1):28–34, 1998.

32. Karch, S.B., Green, G.S. et al. Myocardial hypertrophy and coronary artery disease in male cocaine users. *J. Forensic Sci.* 40(4):591–595, 1995.

33. Wiener, R.S., Lockhart, J.T., and Schwartz, R.G. Dilated cardiomyopathy and cocaine abuse: report of two cases. *Am. J. Med.* 81:699–701, 1986.

7

MEDICO-LEGAL INVESTIGATION OF DEATHS DUE TO EXCITED DELIRIUM SYNDROME

The two most important functions of a medico-legal office are the determination of the cause and manner of death. Deaths handled by these offices generally fall into three categories: deaths due to violence, suspicious deaths, and sudden and unexpected deaths. Deaths due to excited delirium syndrome fall under the jurisdiction of medico-legal systems because of the suspicion that the cause of death is violence.

Because of the circumstances surrounding deaths due to excited delirium, there are often charges of police or medical misconduct. In some cases, allegations of murder are made. When no physical cause for the death is found at autopsy, this is ascribed to a cover-up. The problem with excited delirium syndrome is that the cause of death is complex. It is the consequence of a combination of the normal physiologic changes seen in a struggle and, depending on the case, the use of illicit drugs, medications, and natural disease. The public and the media, however, are looking for simple answers. They assume that such deaths must be the result of misconduct by police and/or medical personnel. That death can be due to the normal physiological reactions of the body to stress gone awry, and the use of stimulants, does not conform to the present mind-set of many Americans: any time tragedy occurs, someone must be at fault and that person should be punished, or even better, sued.

Farnham and Kennedy[1] feel that the problem with the view of death due to excited delirium by the legal system, the public, and the press is that "Legal reasoning favors single proximate causes rather than medical conditions, but the intervention most proximate to the time of death is not necessarily the cause of death."[1] What these groups are doing is confusing proximity of an action with causality, an error in logic identified by Aristotle more than 2300 years ago. "Compounding the situation is that popular journalism favors controversy and blame rather than balance and exploration."[1]

As noted, two of the most important functions of the medical examiner's or coroner's office are the determination of the cause and manner of death. Clinicians, lawyers, and the lay public often have difficulty understanding the difference between cause of death, mechanism of death, and manner of death. The cause of death is any injury or disease that produces a physiological derangement in the body that results in the individual dying. Examples of cause of death are a gunshot wound of the head, a stab wound of the chest, and coronary artery disease. The mechanism of death is the physiological derangement produced by the cause of death that results in death. Examples of the mechanism of death are hemorrhage, septicemia, and cardiac arrhythmia. The manner of death explains how the cause of death came about. Manners of death are generally considered to be natural, homicide, suicide, accident, and undetermined.

Determination of the cause and manner of death by a forensic pathologist is based on an investigation of the circumstances leading up to and surrounding the death, the past medical history of the deceased, the findings at autopsy, and the results of laboratory tests. No matter how the case presents, it is always best to treat cases of excited delirium syndrome as if one is dealing with a homicide in which there will be subsequent judicial proceedings. It is always better to do too much in such cases than too little.

THE INVESTIGATION

1. A complete investigation of the circumstances leading to and surrounding the death should be conducted. The actions of the individuals involved prior to, at, and after the death should be determined. Police reports of the incident, including copies of interviews with the police officers involved, witnesses, and medical personnel, should be obtained. The forensic pathologist should obtain as much information and as many different accounts of the incident as possible.
2. If the body is still at the scene, a scene investigation should be conducted and photographs be taken. If the scene of the death is a public area and the body has been moved, a scene visit is less significant.

3. All medical records of the deceased should be obtained and reviewed. This includes emergency medical services and hospital records of the fatal event as well as old records. A list of any medications the deceased was taking should be obtained. The strength of the medications, the frequency of their use, and whether the patient was compliant with the instructions about taking the drugs should be determined. Pharmacy records will tell if the individual was taking the medications regularly and at appropriate intervals. The drugs should be researched to see if they affect the autonomic nervous system or cause prolongation of the QT interval.

4. The results of any police laboratory examinations should be obtained.

5. If the individual was hospitalized, any blood taken on admission to the hospital should be sought.

THE AUTOPSY

1. Prior to the autopsy, the forensic pathologist should know the circumstances of the death in as much detail as it is possible to obtain at the time. The pathologist should review all available medical records and, subsequently, should be provided with and review any additional records.

2. The autopsy should be performed by or under the direct supervision of an experienced forensic pathologist, board-certified in anatomical and forensic pathology by the American Board of Pathology.

3. A complete autopsy should be conducted. This should include a detailed examination of the external aspects of the body for evidence of disease or trauma as well as an examination of the clothing. All injuries should be specifically located on the body, described in detail, measured, and photographed. Photographs of the body should be taken even in the absence of injuries so as to document their absence.

4. The internal examination of the body should include examination of all three body cavities, i.e., the cranial cavity, the thorax, and the abdomen. The neck organs, including the tongue, should be removed and examined in detail. When it is felt necessary by the pathologist, additional incisions and examinations should be made. Any trauma noted should be described in detail, measured, and photographed. All evidence of trauma or disease should be described in detail.

5. At the time of autopsy, tissue should be retained from all the major organs for microscopic examination. Microscopic sections of all the

major organs should be made. At least six sections of heart should be examined with at least one coming from the area of the conduction system. All microscopic slides and paraffin blocks should be retained indefinitely. Tissue removed at autopsy should be retained for 5 years.

6. When the pathologist feels it necessary, the brain may be retained for subsequent examination by a neuropathologist.

7. Genetic testing may be considered if a condition such as the prolonged QT syndrome is suspected.

TOXICOLOGY

In cases of death due to excited delirium syndrome, the results of toxicologic testing are extremely important. Toxicologic analyses should be performed on all cases and should be extremely thorough. Thus, a drug such as albuterol, which usually is of little significance, must be sought, as it has effects on blood potassium levels. The toxicology test results should be correlated with the medical history of the deceased, the autopsy findings, and the circumstances leading up to and/or surrounding the death to determine whether a drug was a cause of death, a contributory factor, or played no role.

1. In all cases, it is recommended that at the minimum, blood, vitreous, urine, and bile be obtained for toxicological analysis.

2. All specimens should be collected with a clean needle and a new syringe.

3. The specimens of blood, urine, bile, and vitreous should be placed in glass containers, not plastic. This is because these fluids can leach out plastic polymers from the wall of a plastic container. If the blood is subsequently analyzed by gas chromatography, the polymers will give peaks that may mask certain compounds and interfere with analysis. In some cases, substances such as volatiles can be lost due to absorption by the plastic.

4. The blood should be collected from the femoral vessels. If blood cannot be collected from these vessels, then the other sites for collection in descending order of preference are as follows:
   a. The subclavian vessels
   b. The root of the aorta
   c. The pulmonary artery
   d. The superior vena cava
   e. The heart

5. A minimum of 50 ml of blood should be collected:
   a. 20 ml in a 20-ml red-top glass test tube

    b. 20 ml in two 10-ml gray-top glass test tubes (preservative potassium oxalate and sodium fluoride)

    c. 10 ml in a purple top glass test tube (preservative EDTA)

6. All the vitreous should be collected.
7. 20 ml of urine should be collected.
8. Up to 20 ml of bile should be collected.
9. The specimens should be labeled with the name of deceased; case number; date of examination; name of the pathologist, and, in the case of the blood, the source of the blood, e.g., the femorals.
10. If the blood is to be analyzed for volatiles, then some of it should be kept in a test tube with a Teflon-lined screw top rather than a rubber stopper, through which volatile compounds can diffuse.
11. If the individual was hospitalized, any blood taken on admission to the hospital should be sought and obtained.

The practice of opening the pericardial sac, positioning a tube or jar under the heart, then cutting the heart and letting blood drain into the receptacle should be condemned, because it *is very easy* to contaminate the contents of the jar with pericardial fluid and other material that may be present in the chest cavities. This may dilute the blood (with resultant fallacious low levels) or, if there has been diffusion of a drug from the stomach into pericardial or chest fluid, this may actually contaminate it with the drug such that inaccurately high levels are detected in the heart blood.

Blood is preferentially collected from the femoral and subclavian vessels to prevent the possibility and/or contention of postmortem release (redistribution) artifacts. In the case of certain drugs, postmortem levels in heart blood have been challenged on the basis of postmortem drug redistribution. The best examples are the tricyclic antidepressants.

In individuals who have died after several hours or days of hospitalization, one would expect that any drugs in the blood at the time of admission would be metabolized. This is usually but not always the case. In these instances, not only should blood be obtained at autopsy, but the hospital in which the individual was a patient should be contacted to see if any blood obtained at or shortly after hospitalization is still in existence. This should then be obtained for toxicologic analysis.

The tissue of most importance for analysis is blood. This is logical when one realizes that it is the blood level of the drug that has the effect on the individual. A drug detected in the urine or bile had an effect on the individual but one cannot say that it is having an effect at the time the patient died. Thus, toxicologic analysis should be oriented to analysis of blood. With rare exception, virtually all drugs and their major metabolites can now be detected in blood in any modern toxicology lab.

After blood, vitreous humor is next in value. Allowing for appropriate distribution ratios, vitreous reflects the drugs and their levels in the blood 1 to 2 hours prior to death. Virtually any drug detectable in the blood is detectable in the vitreous if one uses analytical techniques and equipment of sufficient sensitivity. The significance of the level present is another matter. Vitreous is analyzed for alcohol when a positive blood alcohol is obtained, as this reflects the blood alcohol level 1 to 2 hours prior to death.

Most drugs are excreted in the urine. Analysis of urine for drugs is easy because there is no protein binding to hinder extraction and many drugs are concentrated in the urine. It has to be realized, however, that the level of a drug in the urine is usually of no significance in the interpretation of the cause of death. It is the level in the blood that determines whether an individual lives or dies.

After one analyzes the specimens, one should keep the residual specimens a minimum of 2 to 5 years.

CERTIFICATION OF DEATH

Following the autopsy, if there is no evidence of sufficient trauma to explain death, this information should be released to the public. No ruling regarding the cause of death should ever be made until all the investigating and testing are complete.

After completion of the investigation, the autopsy, toxicology, and any additional testing, a ruling on the cause and manner of death should be made. If death is due to excited delirium syndrome, the certification of the cause and manner of death is then made. There are two common ways of certifying the cause of death. First is to sign out the cause of death as excited delirium. The "struggle" and other factors such as cocaine intoxication can be designated as contributory causes. The other way is to sign out the cause of death in a descriptive manner, e.g., "Cardiopulmonary arrest during violent struggle in individual under influence of cocaine, alcohol, etc." In individuals with psychoses, this is listed either as a contributory cause or incorporated in the descriptive diagnosis. Local custom may determine how the cause of death is designated.

Designation of manner of death is more difficult. Because of the effects of a struggle, one cannot classify a case of excited delirium syndrome as a natural death. One is then left with homicide or accident. Since a violent struggle has occurred with interaction between two or more individuals, the best classification of the manner of death is probably homicide. A good argument for an accident can be made, however. It is at this point that local custom may determine how the manner of death is designated. If the case is called a homicide, one must explain to the public and press that the designation of the case as a homicide does not indicate that there was necessarily any criminal activity involved, that there is a difference between homicide and murder. It is more important to certify the cause of death in cases of excited delirium syndrome than the manner of death.

REFERENCE

1. Farnham, F.R and Kennedy, H.G. Acute excited states and sudden death: much journalism, little evidence. *Br. Med. J.* 315(7116):1107–1108, 1997.

General Reference

Di Maio, V.J.M. and Di Maio, D.J. *Forensic Pathology*, 2nd ed. CRC Press, Boca Raton, FL, 2001.

8

CASES OF EXCITED DELIRIUM SYNDROME

The following cases of excited delirium syndrome are presented from the authors' files. In none of these cases was the deceased hog-tied. In all instances where handcuffs were used, the hands were cuffed behind the back. None of these individuals was obese unless so indicated, and none was wedged in an environment that would restrict respiration. If body temperature was taken at or immediately after the arrest, it is so noted. Petechiae were sought in all cases but are mentioned only if present. All but two of the cases were autopsied by either one of the authors (V.D.M.) or a forensic pathologist working in his office.

EXCITED DELIRIUM SYNDROME ASSOCIATED WITH MENTAL ILLNESS AND NATURAL DISEASE

Case 1

The deceased was a 45-year-old white male, manager of a company on the U.S.–Mexico border, who for 4 to 5 days preceding his death had experienced paranoid delusions and hallucinations. On the day of his death, he ran hysterically toward the U.S. Customs area on the border between Mexico and Texas. The Customs agents attempted to calm him down. He became combative, was handcuffed, and then placed on the ground. He developed seizures and the emergency medical service (EMS) was summoned. On arrival of the EMS, he had no vital signs. CPR was unsuccessful.

At autopsy, he was a slightly obese white male with minor contusions and abrasions of the body. The brain demonstrated a thin subdural film of blood over the right parietal and occipital lobes, some patchy subarachnoid hemorrhage, but no brain swelling. The brain was examined by a neuro-pathologist who concluded that the changes noted were either agonal or a postmortem artifact, of no significance and not contributory to the death. The rapidity of the death also negates attributing any significance to the findings in the head. The heart was mildly enlarged, weighing 430 g, with mild left ventricular hypertrophy and a single focus of 80% narrowing of the right coronary artery — 70 to 75% narrowing of a coronary artery is significant and can cause a fatal cardiac arrhythmia. Toxicology disclosed a low therapeutic level (0.06 mg/l) of amitriptyline. It was felt that the coronary artery disease in this individual was a contributing factor to the death.

Case 2

The deceased was an obese 16-year-old black female with a history of recurrent depression. At the time of her death, she was a patient in a mental institution. She saw another patient being restrained and went to her aid. She was described as extremely violent. The staff placed her in a basket hold, and took her to the floor. She was given a 50-mg intra-muscular (IM) injection of Thorazine. There was no compression of her trunk. Approximately 10 minutes later, she stopped struggling. She was then carried to an isolation room. She was noted to be breathing and have eye movement at the time. When checked several minutes later, she was found unresponsive.

At autopsy, there were no injuries. She was 66 inches tall and weighed 244 lb. Her heart was enlarged, weighing 330 g (mean heart weight in women 15 to 19 years is 232 g with a standard deviation of 43 g in the authors' experience).* A complete toxicology screen was positive for fluoxetine (0.46 mg/l); norfluoxetine (1.3 mg/l), and trace amounts of chlorpromazine. A subsequent investigation revealed that her father had died of Wolfe-Parkinson-White syndrome at age 31 years.

In Wolfe-Parkinson-White syndrome, there are congenital conduction abnormalities of the heart that produce arrhythmia. Occasionally, the arrhythmia is fatal. This condition may have been present in the patient, as there is a hereditary tendency, and may have been a contributory factor in the death. The diagnosis can only be made antemortem. In summary, the deceased had enlargement of the heart and a family history of a potentially fatal cardiac condition.

---

* Unpublished study of V.J.M. Di Maio, M.D.

Case 3

The deceased was a 67-year-old white male with a history of bipolar disease who had threatened his relatives. The police had dealt with him before. The situation was usually handled by requesting the deceased to leave, which he would. This time as the officer approached to make this request, the deceased struck him with a telephone and stabbed him in his arm, leg, and abdomen. A violent struggle ensued and the officer wrestled the knife away from the attacker. A second officer arrived at the scene at this time and became involved in the struggle. They were able to roll the individual face down. One officer held him down with his hands while the other placed his knee in the small of his back. At this time, they handcuffed him. By this time, other officers had arrived. They stood the individual on his feet and he walked to a patrol car. They bent him over the hood and searched him. During this time, he continued to yell incoherently and to struggle. As the officers stood him up, he went limp. The officers felt he was just being uncooperative and placed him on the backseat of the car. He did not appear to be in any distress. Several minutes later, he was checked on and found to be unresponsive. At this time, he was still lying on the rear seat. CPR was immediately instituted by EMS workers who were at the scene and he was transported to the hospital. On arrival, he was felt to have irreversible hypoxic encephalopathy. He never regained consciousness and died 16 days later. A drug screen in the hospital was negative. There was a history of hypertension and chronic obstructive pulmonary disease (COPD). At autopsy, there were minor injuries and 50% narrowing of the proximal left anterior descending coronary artery. The pulmonary disease and cardiac findings were felt to be factors in the death.

Case 4

The police were summoned to a complaint of an individual causing a disturbance. On arrival, they found a 49-year-old white male inside a van yelling, throwing things, and kicking the doors. When they confronted him, he assaulted them. He was handcuffed and his ankles bound. He was not hog-tied. He was then carried to a police van and placed in the back. The police then walked away from the van. According to multiple witnesses (including EMS personnel), he continued to shout and kick for several minutes after being placed in the van. One of the officers requested that EMS check on the individual prior to transport to a hospital. When they went to check, they found him unresponsive. CPR was instituted and he was immediately transported to a hospital where he was pronounced dead.

At autopsy, there were multiple contusions and abrasions of the body and bilateral fractures of the superior horns of the thyroid cartilage. There were no scleral or conjunctival petechiae. The airway was patent. The heart was enlarged (490 g) with focal myocardial fibrosis. The liver showed micronodular cirrhosis. A toxicology screen was negative except for marijuana. Investigation revealed a history of bipolar disease with multiple hospital admissions. The fractures of the larynx, which occurred during the struggle with the police, were felt to play no role in this death. The individual was shouting after receiving the injuries, indicating an open airway. In addition, the airway was found to be open at autopsy without swelling or obstruction. The heart disease was felt to be a contributory factor in the death.

Case 5

The deceased was a 29-year-old black male who was observed running down a street screaming incoherently. The officers attempted to subdue the deceased at which time he bit one of them. He pushed away from the officers and jumped into a squad car attempting to grab a shotgun. A violent struggle ensued with use of OC (Pepper) spray. He was handcuffed and placed in a police paddy wagon, sitting upright, held in place by seatbelts. They drove him to a hospital to get him "medically cleared," due to the use of OC spray. When they arrived at the emergency room, the deceased was in complete arrest. Resuscitation was unsuccessful. Witnesses confirmed the accounts of the officers. Family members stated that the deceased had used illicit drugs in the past. There was no known psychiatric history, although a brother was schizophrenic. Toxicological analysis was positive for cannabinoids but negative for cocaine, benzodiazepines, methamphetamines, phencyclidine, or other illicit drugs. The autopsy revealed superficial abrasions and contusions of the body; cardiomegaly (520 g), and sickle cell trait (S-A). The cardiac disease and sickle cell trait were felt to be contributory factors in the death.

Conclusion

In all five cases, excited delirium syndrome was accompanied by significant natural disease that contributed to the death by making the individual more susceptible to a fatal cardiac arrhythmia. Two individuals showed significant coronary atherosclerosis (Cases 1 and 3); the other three, enlargement of the heart. One of three individuals with an enlarged heart showed myocardial fibrosis; another had sickle cell trait and the third might have had congenital malfunction of the conduction system.

EXCITED DELIRIUM SYNDROME ASSOCIATED WITH MENTAL RETARDATION AND OBESITY

Case 6

The deceased was a 37-year-old severely mentally retarded white man with a history of asthma and obesity. While at a community living center, he became agitated and attempted to grab a female employee. The staff attempted to calm the individual verbally but he remained agitated and began to flail his arms about. He dropped to his knees and began to breathe heavily. Another female employee approached him and attempted to calm him. He grabbed her by the hair. A male employee freed her but was struck in the process. The individual began rolling about the floor flailing his arms. He then lay prone on the floor. The employees grabbed his arms and feet and held him in this position. After an unknown period of time, he was noted to be cyanotic. He was rolled onto his back and was found to be without respiration. The staff instituted CPR. On arrival of EMS, he was in asystole. He was transported to the hospital and was admitted in full arrest with ongoing CPR. He was then pronounced dead.

At autopsy he was 60½ inches tall and weighted 240 lb. There were no petechiae of the sclerae or conjunctivae. The heart was normal in size (290 g) with open coronary vessels, except for a focus of 50% narrowing of the left main coronary artery. Microscopic sections of the lungs showed changes consistent with an acute asthmatic attack with scattered bronchial plugs. It was felt that death was due to a combination of excited delirium syndrome, asthma, obesity, focal coronary atherosclerosis, and restraint of an obese individual in the prone position.

Conclusion

It was the authors' opinion that holding this obese individual in a prone position would have impaired respiration and was a contributory factor in the death. Whether this alone in an individual with excited delirium syndrome would have been sufficient to cause death is speculative. In the only other case involving excited delirium syndrome, obesity, and the prone restrained position that the authors have encountered, the individual also had advanced heart disease.

EXCITED DELIRIUM SYNDROME ASSOCIATED WITH MENTAL ILLNESS AND THERAPEUTIC MEDICATIONS

Case 7

The deceased was a 9-year-old white male with bipolar disease and attention deficit disorder who suddenly became violent while in a mental facility. He was brought to the floor and held there for 20 minutes. He was held face down, with one attendant holding his feet and another placing her chest on his back below the shoulder blades. The feet were released twice in approximately 20 minutes. During this time, he would appear to calm down and then become violent again. The female attendant occasionally released the pressure on the back. He appeared to calm and at this point was noted to be unresponsive. EMS was summoned and he was transported to a hospital. He survived approximately 21 hours in the hospital.

At autopsy, there were minor abrasions and contusions. Toxicology on blood obtained at autopsy revealed blood levels of: 0.61 mg/l venlafaxine and 0.20 mg/l amphetamine. Both of these drug levels are in the high therapeutic range in spite of the fact that they represent levels at the time of death — 21 hours plus after the arrest. The blood levels at the time of cardiac arrest would have been significantly higher.

Venlafaxine, like cocaine, is a potent inhibitor of norepinephrine reuptake. Amphetamine is a sympathomimetic causing an increase in blood levels of epinephrine and norepinephrine. In this case, the elevated levels of the two medications present were felt to be cardiotoxic and contributory to the death.

Case 8

The patient was a 30-year-old black male with a history of paranoid schizophrenia who was a patient in a state hospital. He got into a dispute with and attacked a nurse. Additional staff were summoned; 6 to 7 individuals pulled him off the nurse and held him in place on the floor, talking to him. He was held down by his arms and legs. There was no pressure to his torso. He continued to struggle for 5 to 10 minutes during which time he was given four injections, two of Haldol (5 mg each injection) and two of ativan (3 mg each injection) in the buttocks. He eventually stopped struggling. When turned over, he was observed to be in respiratory arrest. He was in asystole on arrival of the EMS. The autopsy was negative.

Toxicology revealed the following blood levels:

Valproic acid	36.2 mg/l
Olanzapine	0.90 mg/l
Venlafaxine	1.5 mg/l
Propranolol	1.1 mg/l

Olanzapine is an antipsychotic medication associated with neuroleptic malignant syndrome. This is a high therapeutic level. Venlafaxine, a potent inhibitor of norepinephrine reuptake, is in a high therapeutic level. Propranolol, a beta receptor blocker, is also at a high therapeutic level.

Conclusion

Many medications used to treat individuals with intrinsic mental disease have cardiotoxic potential. This may vary from prolongation of the QT interval (Haldol) to inhibition of norepinephrine reuptake (venlafaxine).

EXCITED DELIRIUM SYNDROME ASSOCIATED WITH USE OF COCAINE

Case 9

The police responded to a report of an individual running down the street smashing the windows of cars. On arrival, they found a disheveled 27-year-old white male screaming incoherently. As they attempted to apprehend him, he resisted. A violent struggle ensued. It took four officers to pull him to the ground. He continued to resist as they attempted to handcuff him. After a brief but violent struggle, they finally handcuffed him with his hands behind his back. His feet were bound together to stop him from kicking. He was not hog-tied, however. He appeared to quiet down. A minute or two after he stopped resisting, he was observed not to be breathing. EMS was summoned and he was found to be in cardiopulmonary arrest. He was transported to the hospital but never responded to resuscitation. At autopsy, there were a number of minor abrasions and contusions. No natural disease was present. Toxicology revealed a blood cocaine level of 1.0 µg/ml and a benzoylecognine level of 0.82 µg/ml.

Case 10

The police were summoned to a complaint of an individual causing a disturbance. On arrival at 0601 hours, they found that the EMS had also been summoned and were already at the scene. The individual, a 24-year-old white male, was screaming incoherently. The police felt that he was a danger to himself and others and attempted to handcuff him. A violent struggle ensued. The individual was handcuffed and his ankles bound. The police then requested that EMS transport him to the hospital. They refused because he was still yelling and kicking. He began to calm down somewhat and the EMS agreed to transport him but only if an officer was also present in the back of the ambulance. He was placed on a stretcher in the ambulance. On the way to the hospital, he continued to struggle.

Two blocks from the hospital he ceased struggling. The EMS technician noted that he was not breathing and began attending to him. He arrived at the hospital at approximately 0620 hours, 20 minutes after the incident started. He was found to be in asystole and resuscitation was instituted. He was pronounced dead 30 minutes after arrival. At autopsy, there were some minor abrasions and contusions. The cocaine level was 1.4 μg/ml; benzoylecgonine was 1.9 μg/ml.

Case 11

The deceased was a 30-year-old white male who appeared at a neighbor's house agitated, hallucinating, and sweating profusely. The neighbor and his wife tried to calm him down. They took him into a bedroom where a struggle ensued. The neighbors held him down on a bed until he calmed down. They left him in the bedroom kneeling on the floor, his body on the bed, with his eyes open and breathing. When the wife returned to the room, he was in cardiopulmonary arrest. At autopsy, there were multiple, minor contusions. Toxicology revealed a blood cocaine level of 0.48 mg/l; a benzoylecgonine level of 5.16 mg/l, and a dextromethorphan level of 0.16 mg/l.

Case 12

The police responded to a report of a 24-year-old white male running down the street jumping in front of cars. On arrival, they saw the suspect jumping on a truck, screaming incoherently and attempting to knock out its rear window. Two officers attempted to put him in custody and a violent struggle ensued. They were finally able to handcuff him using two pairs of handcuffs. The officers were not in physical contact with the individual after handcuffing him. The individual began striking his head on the pavement, when suddenly he stopped moving. The officers could not get any response and summoned the EMS. On arrival, EMS noted a temperature of 108°F. Resuscitation was instituted and he was air-evacuated to a hospital. On arrival, he was in asystole. Resuscitation was unsuccessful and he was pronounced dead. The time from initial police contact to pronouncement of death was approximately 1 hour and 43 minutes. At autopsy, there were minor abrasions and contusions. Blood cocaine was 0.55 mg/l; benzoylecgonine was 7.18 mg/l.

Case 13

The deceased was a 31-year-old white male whose wife had left him immediately prior to the incident. She stated that he was paranoid, delusional, and "acting weird." He was observed walking down the street shouting irrationally. EMS was summoned, arriving at 0450 hours. On encountering the individual, the EMS personnel called for the police. On arrival of the police, the respondents now consisted of four police officers and two EMS personnel. The EMS personnel attempted to place him on a stretcher to transport him to the hospital. At this time, he began to kick and scream. All six individuals then attempted to control him. A violent struggle lasting 6 to 7 minutes occurred. Eventually, he was handcuffed. At no time during the struggle was pressure applied to his chest or abdomen by either hands or knees. Once cuffed, he started to calm down and then suddenly went limp. He was found to be in cardiopulmonary arrest. CPR was immediately instituted and he was transported to the hospital. On arrival at the hospital, a sinus rhythm was restored. No temperature was obtained on admission. He never regained consciousness and died at 2315 hours, approximately 18 hours after admission.

The autopsy revealed minor abrasions, contusions, and lacerations. The heart was enlarged (450 g) with left ventricular hypertrophy and <20% stenosis of the coronary arteries. Toxicology performed on blood obtained postmortem revealed low levels of cocaine, benzoylecgonine, and coca-ethylene.

Case 14

The police were summoned to a motel because a 34-year-old white male was running around the motel shouting incoherently, disrobing, and scattering his clothing. The officers attempted to restrain the individual. A violent struggle ensued and he was handcuffed. Immediately after the struggle, he became unresponsive. EMS was summoned. He was found to be in asystole and transported to a hospital where he was dead on arrival. Syringes and white powder were found in his motel room. At autopsy, there were some minor abrasions and contusions, with markings on the wrist consistent with handcuffs. The heart was mildly enlarged (410 g) with an atherosclerotic plaque occluding 90% of the lumen of the proximal left anterior descending coronary artery. Toxicology revealed a blood cocaine level of 6.94 mg/l and a benzoylecgonine level of 13.87 mg/l.

Case 15

The deceased was a 34-year-old white male with a history of intravenous drug abuse who appeared to be his usual self prior to going into the bathroom at a relative's house. Shortly after exiting the bathroom, he began punching holes in the walls, turning over furniture, kicking the dog, and chasing an 8-year-old niece. The deceased then left the residence, broke into an adjacent house, and assaulted a 75-year-old resident. He left this residence and, on arrival of the police, was observed crawling down the middle of the street. The two responding officers attempted to restrain the individual, and a violent struggle ensued. They got the individual to the ground and handcuffed him. Immediately following the placement of handcuffs the deceased became unresponsive. The officers removed the cuffs and began CPR. EMS was called. On arrival, the deceased was in asystole. He was transported to the hospital where he was pronounced dead. At autopsy, the deceased was 69 inches tall and weighed 250 lb. There were a number of minor abrasions and contusions of the body. The heart was enlarged, weighing 580 g, but without significant atherosclerosis of the vessels. Microscopic sections of the heart revealed mild focal and interstitial fibrosis. Toxicology revealed a blood cocaine level of 0.53 mg/l and benzoylecgonine of 1.3 mg/l. A used syringe was found at the relative's residence.

Case 16

The deceased was a 26-year-old black male who, according to his wife, began hallucinating after taking some drugs. He left his residence and began running in and out of traffic, talking incoherently, and attempting to get into passing cars. The responding police officers pulled him to the ground and applied handcuffs. At this time, he was described as thrashing about and yelling incoherently. The officers picked him up and began walking him to a police vehicle. At this point, he went limp and fell to the ground. The officers picked him up and he continued to resist. They carried him to the car and put him in the backseat sitting up. All this time, he continued to struggle. As an officer placed a hobble restraint around his ankles, he ceased to struggle and stopped breathing. The officers knew immediately something was wrong. They took him out of the vehicle, removed the cuffs, and began CPR. EMS was summoned and he was transported to the hospital where he was pronounced dead. His temperature in the emergency room was 105.2°F.

At autopsy, there were minor abrasions of the right side of the face and tip of the shoulder. Occasional petechiae of the sclera and conjunctivae were present. Blood recovered at autopsy revealed a cocaine level of 0.2 µg/ml and a benzoylecgonine level of 2.6 µg/ml.

Case 17

The police were summoned to a report of a domestic disturbance. On arrival, a 34-year-old white male was observed to be shouting hysterically, running about, sweating profusely, and appeared to be under the influence of drugs. A struggle with the police ensued. He was handcuffed, shackles were applied, and he was transported to the nearest hospital. On arrival, he was aggressive, shouting and violently struggling. He was placed face down on a gurney and tied down by the nursing staff. Because of his violent struggling, the nurses requested that the handcuffs and shackles be left in place. He was then examined by a physician. He continued to struggle. A nurse gave him 5 mg of Haldol and 2 mg of ativan IM. Approximately 15 minutes later, he was noted to be not moving or breathing and in cardiac arrest. The restraints were removed and resuscitation begun. Cardiac rhythm returned but he had suffered irreversible cerebral hypoxia. He died in the hospital approximately 12 hours after the police responded to the scene.

At autopsy, there were minor abrasions and contusions. The heart was mildly enlarged weighing 420 g and showed left ventricular hypertrophy. Blood removed at autopsy revealed a cocaine level of 0.12 µg/ml and a 8.2 µg/ml level of benzoylecgonine.

Case 18

The deceased was a 27-year-old white male with a history of drug abuse. He entered a neighbor's residence where he began "trashing" it. The neighbors subdued the individual tying his hands and feet with rope. They then summoned the EMS and police. On arrival, they found him bound, lying on the floor, mumbling incoherently, and struggling. The struggling was so violent that the EMS personnel asked the police to assist in restraining the individual as they began to examine him. As they began the examination, he suddenly went limp and was asystolic. Resuscitation was begun and he was transported to the hospital where he was dead on arrival.

At autopsy, he had an enlarged heart (470 g) with biventricular hypertrophy. The blood cocaine level was 0.01 µg/ml and the benzoylecgonine level was 3.6 µg/ml.

Case 19

The deceased was a 29-year-old white male involved in a police chase. After crashing his car, he attempted to flee on foot but was apprehended after a violent struggle. While fleeing, he was witnessed to have been snorting a white substance, later determined to be cocaine. The individual was described as combative, screaming, spitting, yelling, not answering questions, and attempting to assault the police. He was handcuffed and placed in the rear of a patrol car where he continued to struggle. He was noted to be "banging" his head against the window of the car and kicking the roof.

At 1248 hours, approximately 35 minutes after the chase began, the police arrived at a magistrate's office for booking. After removal from the vehicle, the individual began to walk into the magistrate's office. At this time, he again began to struggle and kick. It took five officers to place him on the ground where he was placed in leg restraints. Because of his weight, and his refusal to walk, he was dragged through the door of the magistrate's office. Once inside, he began to bang his head on the floor. A nurse at the magistrate's office recommended that he be taken to the emergency room of the county hospital. EMS was summoned but refused to transport him because of his extremely violent behavior. He was put in the back of a police car and transported to the hospital. The EMS unit followed.

The patient arrived at the hospital emergency room at approximately 1343 hours. He was placed on a gurney with the help of the police and medical personnel. He continued to struggle violently. His behavior was described as delusional. The patient was positioned face down, on his stomach, with four-point restraint. The nursing staff unsuccessfully attempted to de-escalate the aggression verbally. He was given 4 mg of ativan IM at 1343 hours, 6 mg at 1349, and 2 mg at 1353. At 1352 hours, he was given 5 mg of Haldol IM. There was no evidence that these drugs in any way decreased his excited delirium. He continued to struggle, screaming and ranting when, at 1357 hours, he suddenly became unresponsive with no pulse. Cardiopulmonary resuscitation was instituted. The rectal temperature was 105° F. Cardiac activity eventually returned but he had suffered irreversible hypoxic brain injury and he died 3 days later. The time from the beginning of this incident until death was approximately 1 hour and 44 minutes.

A subsequent autopsy revealed no evidence of significant trauma. It did reveal a massively enlarged heart weighing 600 g. Toxicology confirmed the fact that the deceased had been on cocaine at the time of his arrest. Review of his past medical records revealed a past hospital admission for cocaine intoxication with rhabdomyolysis and acute renal failure. He had made a complete recovery from this incident.

Could the outcome of this case have been different? Possibly. If the deceased had been transported directly from the scene to the hospital, sedation could have been instituted sooner and the physiological cascade that resulted in death aborted. If the EMS had had the power to administer sedative medications, this may also have aborted the death. The other possibility is if, on arrival at the hospital, attempts had been made to administer the drugs intravenously. There was no evidence that these drugs, which were given IM, in any way decreased his excited delirium. This is not surprising in that there would have been insufficient time for these drugs to be absorbed into the bloodstream in levels to have had any effect.

EXCITED DELIRIUM SYNDROME IN ASSOCIATION WITH METHAMPHETAMINE

Case 20

911 received a report of an individual terrorizing his family. On arrival of the police, the individual was found to be running about his residence, overturning furniture, and screaming incoherently. He used his fists to punch out a number of windows. He resisted attempts by officers to handcuff him and he was brought to the ground. It took six officers to restrain and handcuff him. He appeared to quiet down and was then noted to be without respiration. EMS was summoned and he was found to be in cardiopulmonary arrest. He was transported to the hospital but never responded to resuscitation. At autopsy, there were a number of minor abrasions and contusions as well as minor glass cuts of the hands. No natural disease was present. The deceased was not obese. Toxicology revealed a methamphetamine level of 0.8 μg/ml and a 0.12% level of alcohol.

Case 21

The police responded to a call of a domestic dispute between a mother and son. The 28-year-old son had a history of using crystal methamphetamine. On arrival, he began arguing with the officers. As the officers tried to calm him, he shoved his mother to the ground. One of the officers sprayed the son with pepper spray. The son then tackled the officer. Both began rolling about on the ground. The second officer joined the fight. One of the officers tried to use a neck hold. The struggle was too violent and the hold was ineffective. The mother called 911 and additional officers arrived. They handcuffed and shackled the son. Initially he was handcuffed with his hands in front and then placed prone. The cuffs were removed and he was cuffed with his hands behind his back. There appeared to be some resistance to the recuffing. After recuffing, he appeared to become calm. He was then noted to be unresponsive, breathing shallowly, and staring straight ahead. One officer then felt for his carotid pulse. After 2 minutes of monitoring, the pulse could no longer be detected and breathing ceased. The cuffs were removed and CPR instituted.

At autopsy, there were bilateral conjunctival and facial hemorrhages, a contusion of the anterior aspect of the neck, bilateral superior horn fractures of the thyroid cartilage with hemorrhage. There were multiple contusions and abrasions of the body. The methamphetamine level was 0.33 mg/l, amphetamine level was 0.06 mg/l. The fractures of the larynx, which occurred during the struggle with the police, were felt to have played no role in this death. There was no prolonged period of pressure being applied to the neck. The airway was patent.

EXCITED DELIRIUM SYNDROME IN ASSOCIATION WITH OTHER DRUGS

Case 22

The deceased was a 38-year-old black male who had been a client of the Texas Mental Health/Mental Retardation Agency. He burst through the doors of a church during services, yelling and causing a disturbance. Members of the church subdued, handcuffed, and escorted him out of the church. He broke the handcuffs and continued to fight. Two additional pairs of handcuffs were then placed on his wrists. He then quit fighting. At this time, he was noted to be unresponsive. No choke holds were used or blows struck. He was transported to the hospital where he was dead on arrival. At autopsy, there were minor abrasions and a laceration of a finger. Toxicologic analysis of blood revealed 1.4 mg/l diphenhydramine, 0.08 mg/l diazepam, 0.07 mg/l nordiazepam, and marijuana. The heart was mildly enlarged (420 g). Therapeutic blood levels of diphenhydramine (DPH) are generally below 0.12 mg/dl. Thus, the deceased had a markedly elevated level.

In high or toxic levels, DPH can cause excited delirium. In addition, DPH is potentially cardiotoxic by virtue of its ability to produce prolongation of the QRS interval. In this, it is similar to tricyclic antidepressants.

9

PREVENTION OF EXCITED
DELIRIUM SYNDROME:
THE POLICE AND
FIRST RESPONDERS

"The seeds of the future are sown in the present and the directions of their growth and development derive from the past."

— **Lisa Robinson, RN, Ph.D., C.S., F.A.A.N.**

INTRODUCTION

It is not possible to predict when an episode of excited delirium will result in death.

What we do know is that such deaths occur in association with a violent struggle. The struggle is usually initiated when medical or law enforcement personnel attempt to restrain an individual in order to prevent the individual from harming himself or herself or others after all therapeutic measures to defuse the aggressive and violent behavior have failed. Death typically occurs minutes after the *struggle ceases*.

In excited delirium syndrome, there is a synergetic relationship between the physiological effects of the excited delirium, drugs, mental disease, and struggling, with resultant sudden death. Once the "struggle" begins, the cascade of physiological responses precipitated by these factors results in the death. Therefore, de-escalation of the excited delirium, prevention of the struggle, or rapid termination of the physiological effects of the struggle are the best ways to prevent excited delirium syndrome.

Widespread public outcry over the sudden death of individuals in police custody has in some cases produced panicky unscientific suggestions to prevent such deaths or a hunt for scapegoats to blame for the deaths. In some areas of the country, police officers have been accused of killing the individuals by use of inappropriate restraint measures even if there was no evidence that they even employed such procedures. Publications proposing positional asphyxia as the cause of death continue, even though research has discredited the basis for this theory.[1-4] Because of this, techniques to prevent death due to excited delirium syndrome have focused on preventing non-existent restraint/positional asphyxia.

Deaths due to excited delirium syndrome will continue to occur if nothing is changed in the handling and care of individuals experiencing excited delirium. Therefore, the aim of this chapter is to propose practices and procedures that can be used by law enforcement, emergency medical service (EMS), and emergency room personnel to prevent deaths from excited delirium syndrome.

The various theories and methods presented in this chapter have been extracted from the mental health literature in regard to nursing and hospital emergency care as well as from case reports of sudden deaths occurring in the community, emergency room, or psychiatric and medical facilities.

THE PROBLEM

Law enforcement and EMS responders encounter two groups of individuals with excited delirium who may die suddenly from excited delirium syndrome. The first are those individuals whose psychotic behavior is drug or alcohol induced. These are the most commonly encountered and the most likely to die. The second group is composed of the mentally ill who are experiencing a relapse of the psychotic features that are inherent to their mental illness or who may have relapsed due to use of illicit drugs or alcohol. The presenting symptoms of both groups are essentially identical. Police tend to encounter individuals with drug-induced excited delirium more than those suffering from mental illness. Mental illness combined with illicit drug use probably presents the greatest risk for a violent encounter by police or EMS personnel, as patients with mental disorders who use drugs have the highest probability of violent behavior.[5]

The dramatic increase in deaths due to excited delirium syndrome in the community is due to two factors. First is the increased use of illegal stimulants, such as cocaine, since the 1980s. Second is the appearance of large numbers of mentally ill individuals in the community at large. Both factors have increased the number of encounters between the police and individuals with excited delirium, and thus the number of deaths.

Changes in psychiatric care are the cause of increased numbers of the severely mentally ill being on the streets. Historically, care of the mentally ill client occurred in hospital-based facilities. This care was provided by nursing staff and was primarily custodial. Beginning in the late 1940s, detractors of mental hospitals began a campaign to replace them with community-based outpatient treatment facilities.[6] This campaign was aided by the introduction in the 1950s of psychotropic drugs for the treatment of severe mental disease.[7–9] This led to the widespread release of formerly institutionalized patients into the community. Community-based facilities were intended to reduce long-term institutionalization of mentally ill patients and provide comprehensive care focused on prevention and rehabilitation. While marvelous in concept, adequate financing by both the federal and local governments never occurred. Thus, communities now contain large numbers of mentally ill individuals who have stopped taking their medications. If these individuals become a public nuisance or violent, the police are summoned. The mentally ill then end up in either jail or the emergency room of a local hospital. The most common cause of violent behavior in the mentally ill is recurrence of psychotic symptoms due to non-adherence to antipsychotic medications and/or the use of illicit drugs and/or alcohol.[10,11]

LAW ENFORCEMENT

The prevention of deaths due to excited delirium syndrome by the police is somewhat problematic as law enforcement personnel are presented with situations that have greater lethal potential and more unknown elements than those involving mental health facilities. The individuals they encounter who are susceptible to excited delirium syndrome constitute a subgroup of the population that has a greater potential for violence. High-risk factors possessed by this group are chronic use of illicit drugs, a criminal history, a prior history of violence, and possible possession of weapons.

Complicating the situation for the police is the fact that officers are usually unaware of an individual's past medical history, mental history, history of violence, and whether the individual is on drugs. This is in contrast to the psychiatric staff in a mental institution. Here a prior mental health and behavior history provides staff with a measure for violence prevention and safety with potentially violent patients. This is especially true in regard to a history of violence. One of the most important elements in determining if an individual has the potential for violent behavior *is a prior history of violent behavior.*[11–13]

As the concept of excited delirium syndrome and its cause and mechanism of death is unknown to law enforcement officers, their actions in the arrests of violent offenders experiencing excited delirium do not take into account the risk potential for death of these offenders. Their actions, which are derived from police protocol and training, are deficient in mental and behavioral health practices and techniques for the handling of psychotic individuals, whether the psychosis is due to mental disease or abuse of drugs. Their lack of knowledge, and unintentionally inappropriate practices in attempting arrest, may trigger a fatal situation.

A police officer must make rapid assessments of an individual's mental state as it relates to the potential for violence. This is true whether the excited delirium is due to intrinsic mental disease or drugs. Psychiatric assessment skills used to identify behavioral, cognitive, and emotional characteristics that signal the potential for immediate or future violence are not generally taught in law enforcement training programs. Evaluation of a patient's behavior, mood, and affect is a vital part of mental health skills taught to psychiatric medical personnel. The lack of training in mental health issues related to violent offenders, who may or may not have mental illness, is a serious deficiency in the training of police officers who often face such individuals daily in communities. Law enforcement training protocols should incorporate adequate psychiatric mental health training techniques in managing individuals who either have mental illness or may be displaying symptoms of such due to drugs.

The authors watched a video entitled "Verbal Judo" that is commonly used by police training agencies nationwide.[14] This tape is used to show officers how to handle difficult individuals they encounter in communities. While the tape offers some appropriate information, it does not address issues of violence related to mental illness and drug use, which is the key element of sudden deaths in police custody arrests.

The last resort for control of violent behavior by law enforcement is use of physical restraint. This may be preceded by use of chemicals such as pepper spray. In the cases of excited delirium syndrome seen by the authors, the individuals seem unaffected by such chemicals. The only thing that their use seems to accomplish is to increase their aggravation and violence. Taser use is becoming more widespread. Its ability to abort an episode of excited delirium and prevent a death due to excited delirium syndrome is open to question.

In attempting to restrain violent individuals, police endure a significant handicap in that unlike a psychiatric team, which has five to six trained individuals who are called to a code to physically restrain a violent patient, there may only be one or two officers to attempt restraint. Backup support is often not immediately available in many communities because of a lack of officers. Anyone who has ever attempted to physically restrain psychotic violent individuals will tell you how extremely difficult this is and how violently they fight. During this struggle, the individual may be spitting, biting, punching, head butting, kicking, and reaching for whatever is available to harm the officer. Rapid control of this individual is of vital importance to prevent harm to the officers as well as other bystanders.

This violent scene is similar to episodes of excited delirium (commonly referred to as acute psychotic episodes) seen in mental institutions where codes are often called by nursing staff to restrain the violent psychotic patient. The difference is that in mental health facilities the potential for violent behavior may be diffused by other techniques or medication. Whether on the street or in the hospital, however, gaining rapid control of the individual so as to reduce the time of the struggle is of paramount importance in preventing death from excited delirium.

Following a struggle and use of restraint, cardiopulmonary arrest due to excited delirium syndrome may occur at the scene, during transport to jail in a police vehicle, during transport to a hospital by either a police vehicle or EMS, on arrival at a jail or on arrival at the hospital. Typically, these individuals are males between the ages of 16 and 44 years.[15] Most cardiac arrests seem to occur following use of restraint, after the individual stops fighting against the restraint. This would of course correspond to the "period of peril," described by Dimsdale et al.[16] The vast majority of deaths occur at the scene (48%), less commonly during transport (29%), and only occasionally after arrival at a hospital or jail (16%).[15]

If the individual has not arrested at the scene or during transport, upon arrival at the emergency room, the individual is violent, agitated, and fights furiously with medical personnel. The emergency room personnel will maintain restraint and then administer antipsychotic and tranquillizing medications, e.g., lorazepam, intramuscularly. Early intervention by EMS personnel by use of sedative medications at the scene or during transport is usually not provided before arrival at the emergency hospital facility. Rapid administration of sedative medications at the scene may in fact prevent such deaths. The delay in administration of medication at the scene is aggravated by the fact that administration of medication in the emergency room is typically by the intramuscular route, with the associated delay in attaining effective blood levels seen with this route of administration. Giving an injection intravenously in an individual who is fighting furiously is extremely difficult, and may in fact not be feasible, but if possible should occur.

The usefulness of antipsychotic medications, e.g., haloperidol, in these cases is questionable and potentially dangerous. Symptoms of psychotic behavior are usually the result of illicit drug use and not underlying mental disease; therefore, antipsychotic medications are unnecessary. Their use should be considered only after the individual is calm, with stable vital signs and no longer at risk for sudden death due to excited delirium syndrome.

Antipsychotic medications can cause prolongation of the QT interval.[17–21] If given during a time of extreme catecholamine surges, such as occurs during excited delirium, they carry a lethal potential. Prolongation of the QTc interval has been shown to substantially increase the risk of cardiac dysrhythmias. These drugs may be used in association with antidepressants, which also cause prolongation of the QT interval.[17,20]

The authors suggest that the use of antipsychotics for excited delirium be further evaluated. The administration of sedative medications *at the scene* by EMS personnel as a preventive measure against excited delirium syndrome should be explored.

PREVENTION

Material addressing the management and prevention of violent behavior and the potential for death of individuals in excited delirium must be incorporated into educational programs aimed at police, EMS personnel, and emergency room staff. Coordinating and standardizing training programs between medical and law enforcement for identifying symptoms of excited delirium syndrome and instituting prevention strategies within law enforcement agencies nationwide will reduce the potential for such deaths.

To prevent deaths from excited delirium syndrome, the police must:

- Identify individuals in excited delirium
- Attempt to de-escalate the situation and calm them down
- Use overwhelming force if restraint must be used
- After individuals are restrained, monitor them at the scene and during transport
- Immediately transport them to a hospital for treatment and/or observation

Early identification of symptoms and signs present in cases of excited delirium syndrome will provide the police and EMS personnel with a way of detecting potential cases of excited delirium syndrome and, thus, institute measures that can prevent such deaths. The responders can initiate measures aimed at preventing escalation of agitation and violence. Physical intervention should only be a last resort and responders must be prepared for the potential for death to occur.

The presenting behavioral and cognitive symptoms and signs may occur rapidly, and without any noticeable precipitating factors. They may continue to escalate in intensity no matter what is the method of intervention. Behavioral and cognitive indicators for death due to excited delirium syndrome are as follows:

- Extreme agitation and restlessness
- Incoherent and rambling speech
- Hallucinations
- Delusions with paranoid features
- Disorganized thought content
- Bizarre behavior
- Combativeness
- Violence

This behavior may be related to mental illness and/or the use of illicit drugs. Schizophrenia and mania related to bipolar disease have been the most identified mental illnesses associated in death due to excited delirium syndrome. The most common drugs linked to sudden death are methamphetamine and cocaine.

Mental health facilities are designed so as to create the safest possible environment for patients and staff in order to manage the risk potential for violent incidents. In contrast, the police are faced with numerous environmental factors that cannot be anticipated and that may precipitate or escalate a situation into a violent incident. Instead of operating in a safe environment, the police must attempt to create one. If two officers are present, one should be attending to environmental control while the other officer is speaking to the individual. It is important that only one officer directly makes contact verbally with the individual as well as providing a safe physical distance.

Environmental options available to police for prevention of violence include scanning the scene to remove potentially hazardous objects, removing bystanders who might escalate the individual's level of distrust and agitation, and asking others to move away from the individual to reduce stimulation. The police officers should attempt to reduce the noise level. If there is loud music playing at the scene, they should have it shut off.

An individual in acute psychosis is not experiencing reality; therefore, responders should make simple demands stated in a non-challenging manner. Listen patiently for individual response and note the level of acceptance and behavior change. At all times, communicate the willingness to help this individual regain control by statements such as "You seem upset," "We can help," "I'm here to help you," "You are safe."[23] Complement the individual's ability to maintain control and follow instructions. Offer positive feedback as the individual begins to respond in a positive manner. Individuals may pace back and forth or simulate a rocking behavior. This behavior is an attempt to reduce their agitation and should not be stopped but only watched if no violent act is imminent. Offering a cigarette to them if they smoke often will help them calm down and regain control.

Individuals who are psychotic are distrustful. Any form of crowding by attempting to surround them by officers will only escalate their already distrustful, agitated state. Make slow movements, give simple commands; wait and note the individuals' behavioral response. Do they cooperate? Is their level of agitation increasing? Scan the environment for anyone that may have a good rapport with the individual to assist. Establishing rapport and gaining trust in caring for mentally ill patients are components in psychiatric nursing. *If a struggle with a violent individual can be avoided,* death from excited delirium syndrome is avoided.

If the need to physically restrain an individual cannot be avoided by other interventions, restraint must occur rapidly to reduce the time of struggle. Law enforcement personnel should adopt the approach followed by psychiatric staff in gaining rapid control of violent patients. Five to six individuals are utilized to rapidly control the individual. Police officers may be alone or in pairs when responding to disturbances in communities. Backup support may not be available. Because of this, rapid restraint of an individual may not be possible.

Any attempt to restrain or gain physical control of a highly agitated and aggressive individual suffering from excited delirium brings with it the possibility of death. Struggling with individuals in the throes of excited delirium in order to restrain them can last as long as 30 minutes.

The majority of reported sudden deaths in nationwide studies occurred within minutes to 1 hour from initial time of struggle. No reported cases survived after experiencing cardiac arrest, **even when emergency personnel were present and advanced life support was started**.[2,15]

Quick physical control can only be gained by use of overwhelming force. A trained team of medical and law enforcement personnel experienced in physical restraint procedures should be called to the scene prior to attempting physical restraint of individuals in excited delirium. This team can provide psychiatric assessment, rapid medication, and life support if an arrest occurs at the scene. By reducing the time of struggle, and providing immediate sedative medication, the effects of the continued physiological catecholamine surge inherent in the struggle will be reduced and death may be prevented.

At all times, at the scene or during transport, **face-to-face monitoring** of the individual's breathing status **must be done by police or EMS personnel until arrival at a hospital facility**. The individual should be transported in an upright, a seated, or a side-lying position. The authors feel that in virtually all cases, extreme obesity being an exception, the position of the individual during restraint and transport plays no role in causing death. Use of the aforementioned positions is recommended only so that, if death does occur, use of these positions is a defense against an accusation of positional/restraint asphyxia.

If an individual arrests at the scene or during transport, immediate CPR, and electrocardioconversion should be initiated prior to arrival at the emergency room. If no cardiac response is obtained, the use of vasopressin has been shown to demonstrate a greater success in resuscitation of asystolic cardiac arrest than epinephrine.[24,25] The standard guideline for cardiac arrest has been the use of epinephrine as the vasoactive drug of choice in asystolic cardiac arrest. Epinephrine has been demonstrated in clinical research to consume oxygen unlike vasopressin, which increases oxygen to the myocardium. In excited delirium, there is a rapid and tremendous surge of catecholamines, epinephrine, and norepinephrine. The consumption of oxygen during this state of excited delirium further stresses the cardiac response. By virtue of these recent studies, it seems best that if chemical stimulation of the heart is required that the drug used be vasopressin rather than epinephrine.

The problems in the handling of cases by police and EMS fall into five general areas:

1. Lack of training in identifying characteristics of individuals at high risk for death due to excited delirium syndrome
2. Lack of personnel to provide rapid physical restraint so as to reduce time of struggle with an individual — ideally, a minimum of five to six individuals is necessary for rapid physical restraint
3. The inability to provide sedative medications at the scene prior to transport by emergency responders, thus, increasing the time of struggle by that spent in transport to hospital facilities for treatment
4. Lack of nationwide standardization of training programs in violence prevention and management by law enforcement and emergency personnel
5. Lack of nationwide standardization of approved procedures for restraining violent individuals within communities by law enforcement and emergency personnel

Overall, there is a lack of coordination, teaching, and input from community mental health services, law enforcement offices, emergency medical services, and emergency hospital facilities as well as medical examiner's offices in death prevention from excited delirium syndrome. Early identification and intervention equates to death prevention from excited delirium syndrome.

EMERGENCY RESPONDERS

EMS personnel members, like the police, are routinely faced with managing, treating, and transporting violent patients. They as well as emergency room staff are often the recipients of violent attacks from these individuals; 0.8% and 5.0% of all incidents responded to by EMS involved violence or the threat of violence.[10] Often, these violent incidents involve individuals who are mentally ill and/or on alcohol or drugs. While the risk for violence is ever present, only 25% of EMS personnel members considered themselves adequately trained to make assessments of violence.[26] In a survey by the National Association of EMS Physicians, only 47% of EMS agencies have any protocol for managing violent individuals.[26]

EMS personnel have been taught that deaths in association with excited delirium are due to positional asphyxia from improper use of restraints and/or positioning of patients. Therefore, measures to prevent such deaths are focused on preventing this non-existent asphyxia.

In reported cases of excited delirium syndrome where EMS personnel were either present at the scene or responded within minutes and employed current advanced cardiac life support (ACLS) methods for sudden cardiac arrest, no individuals survived.[2] In occasional cases, there is return of cardiac activity but invariably the individual is found to have suffered hypoxic encephalopathy and dies a few days after the original event.

There are two possibilities to explain the fact that cardiopulmonary resuscitation is invariably unsuccessful even if it is instituted immediately. The first is that cardiopulmonary arrest due to excited delirium syndrome is irreversible; the second is that the methods being used to revive individuals with excited delirium syndrome are not effective.

Because, they do not know what has triggered the physiological mechanisms causing the cardiac arrest, EMS personnel members respond to the cardiac arrest with the usual ACLS protocol, which was intended principally for cardiac arrest from heart disease. Epinephrine is a first-line medication for cardiac resuscitation.[24] However, its use in cardiac arrest due to excited delirium syndrome may not only be useless, but potentially harmful. It may increase the probability of death because excited delirium syndrome is characterized by a hyperadrenergic state. Administering epinephrine may be the equivalent of pouring gasoline on a fire.

While no research to date has been conducted regarding the use of an alternative to epinephrine for excited delirium syndrome, specifically, there has been some work of a more general nature. Vasopressin has been shown to demonstrate a greater success in resuscitation of asystolic cardiac arrest than epinephrine.[24,25] Epinephrine causes increased consumption of oxygen by the myocardium while vasopressin increases oxygen to the myocardium. In excited delirium, there is a rapid and tremendous surge of catecholamines, epinephrine, and norepinephrine. The "additional exogenous epinephrine could be expected to exacerbate hypoxemia and advancing acidosis, both of which would be expected to further impair the vasopressor effects of epinephrine as well. Thus, epinephrine might not only be ineffectual, but also potentially detrimental in early asystolic cardiac arrest."[24]

The **timing of sedation** is a critical component in death prevention. The level of agitation that initiates the cascade of physiological events resulting in sudden cardiac arrest must be stopped. Waiting until an individual reaches an emergency room before beginning medication, assuming that the individual lives that long, is foolish. This is especially true, as reversal of the cardiac arrest due to excited delirium syndrome is rare and when it does occur results in hypoxic encephalopathy and death a few days after the original event. The only way to avoid the delay in sedation of individuals in excited delirium is to authorize EMS personnel to administer sedative medication at the scene.

POLICE AND EMS AT THE SCENE

The following actions are recommended for all police and EMS personnel responding to a violent individual who exhibits signs of excited delirium:

- If the first responders are police officers, as soon as it is apparent that the individual is in excited delirium, they should summon EMS and request backup. If the first responders are EMS, they should summon the police, explaining the situation.
- Appoint one individual, either a police officer or an EMS worker, to attempt verbal intervention techniques in order to defuse the situation. This individual should have training in these techniques by approved providers of violence management programs. The police agency and EMS administrators should decide who in the community should receive this training. All conversation with the patient should be with this one individual. The other team members should be securing the scene and standing by to begin a fast physical restraint if it becomes necessary.
- Members of the team should remain calm even if the individual is screaming insults. The ability to be confident and in self-control helps provide "external security" for an individual who is out of control. Psychotic and highly agitated individuals will often have racing thoughts and may not hear your statements. Remain calm and restate requests until compliance is attained. Be patient. Do not take any action unless there is an immediate threat to the individual or others.
- Do not have discussions and arguments within the team regarding what is to be done and who should do it. Plan ahead for procedures. Disagreements within the team only serve to heighten the atmosphere of agitation already present.

- If confronted with a patient with a weapon, the police have to decide whether there is imminent danger. A weapon completely changes the situation. The police officers may have to resort to physical force including lethal force to protect themselves and others. If the police believe that negotiations can still continue, ask politely, never demand, that the individual place the weapon down and move away from it. Never have the individual place it in your hand. Continue to convey to the individual the importance of safety for yourself and the individual in your ability to provide medical care. Be aware of subtle changes in the individual's movements and mental status.

- Statements should always be phrased in a positive manner with offers to help and assist. Never lie unless it is absolutely necessary. If the individual discovers you have lied before being secured, the individual may react with extreme violence.

- Always be direct with statements without becoming confrontational. Be patient. It takes time for a highly agitated individual to calm down. If there is no immediate danger to the individual or yourself, allow space and time for the individual to "vent" and diffuse his or her agitation. This will often help the individual calm down.

- Try to get the individual to sit down. If people sit down, they most likely will calm down.

- Keep a safe distance, 10 to 15 feet from the individual. Never turn your back on a violent psychotic individual. If you need help, back away facing the individual. Know where the individual is at all times.

- Do not maintain eye contact continually as paranoid individuals may interpret this as a threatening behavior to them.

- If working with EMS who can give sedative medications, have the medications prepared before you begin physical restraint. One team member can be doing this while the other is trying to defuse the individual. Offer the individual oral medication initially. At first, the individual will most likely be too mentally impaired to respond to your request. After the individual regains composure, the individual may agree to take the medications offered.

- Remember that individuals with psychotic disorders are mentally impaired and when highly agitated will not comply unless they can be calmed. Highly agitated individuals who are not psychotic can make rational decisions and can be more dangerous than psychotic individuals. They may not back down when confronted with authority. They may be in a rage related to drug use or family conflicts. They will utilize any means of manipulative behavior to gain control of you and others at the scene.

- Maintain your safety and the safety of any people in the environment. Ask other people to leave the scene. Often another party will increase or be the cause of the agitation. Sometimes, another individual or family member who has gained rapport with the individual can assist you in calming the individual down.

- Remove any items in the immediate area that can be used as a weapon if possible. Attempt to move into a safe area, which is open, allows for physical retreat, without interference of objects and individuals when verbal or physical intervention is begun.

- If a verbal intervention does not work, then one must resort to restraint. The police may want to initially try to immobilize the individual with chemicals, e.g., pepper spray. This may or may not work. The authors are aware of numerous cases where chemicals have had absolutely no effect or increased the violence. The use of Tasers in these situations is still being explored.

- If physical restraint has to be employed, it should be overwhelming. The objective is to reduce the time of struggle, thus reducing catecholamine production. At least five to six people should be available to physically restrain an individual in excited delirium. The presence of five to six people as a" show of force" may stop the mentally coherent individual, but not the psychotic one. Having five to six individuals available for physical restraint allows for rapid control and reduction in time of struggle.

- Place the restrained individual in a "side-lying" recumbent position. This provides monitoring of airway and breathing. Arms and feet are secured by applying body pressure to the shoulders and above the knees. Another team member should secure the head to prevent biting. Placing an individual in the "side-lying" position, in itself, will not decrease the probability of cardiopulmonary arrest. However, it will be useful in countering claims of "positional asphyxia" if death due to excited delirium occurs.

- Total physical restraint control should occur in just a few minutes. All team members should be providing continuing monitoring for any signs of changing respiration, or diminished mental status. During the heighten atmosphere of attempting to physically restrain a very violent and angry person, it is not uncommon to get lost in the procedure and forget to monitor for changes in health status. Is the person speaking, screaming, or moaning? If people are speaking, they are also breathing even if they don't make sense. If they were able to formulate statements and questions before you attempted to restrain them, has this changed? Is their speech slurred with unrecognizable statements?

- Once the individual is secure at the scene, the individual should be immediately transported to a hospital. Before transport in the ambulance, administration of a rapid sedative is recommended. Intravenous administration produces the most rapid sedation. Lorazepam is the sedative medication of choice in emergency situations.[5,27] It can be given orally, intramuscularly, or intravascularly. Rapid sedation of aggression and agitation is a primary tool in prevention of death from excited delirium syndrome. Therefore, route of administration should be intravascular if possible. Intramuscular injections are often used first by emergency and psychiatric personnel; however, in cases of excited delirium sudden death occurs within minutes "after" the struggle ceases. If engaging in a struggle cannot be prevented, it is vitally important to reduce the time of agitation and duration of struggle in these individuals. The duration of struggle is related to the rise and fall of catecholamines and sudden death from excited delirium.
- Authorization for the use of sedative medication should be approved prior to attempting restraint.
- At all times, continue to monitor and assess vital signs. Any diminished respiratory status or rapid elevation of core body temperature may signal a danger warning for sudden cardiac arrest from excited delirium syndrome.
- Be ready to immediately begin cardiac resuscitation procedures by use of vasopressin and/or electrocardiac conversion.
- Transport all individuals experiencing excited delirium to a hospital, even if they appear to be recovering.

In preparation for the aforementioned actions, a **Psychiatric Emergency Response Team (PERT)** might be constituted within police departments. Such a team would be formed in conjunction with the EMS. It could be called upon to respond to situations where officers, after attempting preventive measures of de-escalation, need to employ physical restraint. This team would comprise five to six individuals from law enforcement and EMS. The team would be able to assist in the physical restraint of individuals as well as to immediately institute lifesaving measures if cardiac arrest occurs. The need for five to six individuals is based on experience by psychiatric teams used for codes for violent, mentally ill patients in mental institutions. A nurse might also be part of the team.

EMERGENCY ROOMS

Individuals in the throes of excited delirium are increasingly presenting to emergency rooms, either voluntarily or involuntarily after having been transported to the emergency room by either the police or EMS. In some cases, patients will develop excited delirium in the emergency room while there for other health problems. The excited delirium can be due to use of illegal stimulants and/or to intrinsic mental disease.

The management of these patients is the responsibility of the physicians and nurses in the emergency room. Often, this staff must make rapid physical, psychiatric, and behavioral assessments. Treatment procedures for mentally ill patients are not their area of expertise; therefore, they are usually at a disadvantage when confronted with an aggressive individual in excited delirium. They may have little or no knowledge of sudden death occurring during restraint, let alone excited delirium syndrome. The management of violent behavior in patients is initially directed at the use of physical restraints and then pharmacological sedation. Physical restraint is used to protect the individual and the medical personnel from violence; to administer medications, and to be able to perform diagnostic tests. Unfortunately, use of restraints triggers the physiological cascade that can result in sudden death.

No specific pharmacologic treatments are available to treat violent behavior in emergency departments. Typically, the patient is given an antipsychotic medication and a tranquilizer (sedating agent). The most commonly used drugs are lorazepam (a benzodiazepam) and haloperidol.[28] Both drugs can be given orally, intramuscularly, and intravenously. The usual route of administration is intramuscular. Unfortunately, response to intramuscular administration of sedative medication such as lorazepam is in the range of 15 to 30 minutes, minimally. In cases of sudden death due to excited delirium syndrome, the individuals often go into cardiac arrest before the medication can be effective. The route of choice in these patients should be intravenous, for rapidly acting sedation. Unfortunately, because of violent struggling it is often not possible to give drugs intravenously.

Haloperidol, like lorazepam is also given intramuscularly. It also has a significant delay time before producing an effect. In addition, it has the potential to cause prolongation of the QT interval, predisposing patients to sudden cardiac death. This attribute is even worse if it is given intravenously.[21] If the patient is on another medication that also predisposes him or her to QT prolongation, such as a tricyclic antidepressant or erythromycin, there may be potentiation of the effects of haloperidol on QT prolongation.

It is not necessary during an episode of excited delirium to treat the underlying psychosis, if present, by the use of antipsychotic medications. This concept may appear strange to those medical personnel who have always used antipsychotics to reduce psychosis and agitation. There is in fact no immediate urgency in treating an underlying psychosis. The immediate medical problem is not the psychosis but the violent behavior of the individual and the possibility of sudden death. The other fact to remember is that most individuals in excited delirium have this condition due to use of illicit drugs and not underlying mental disease. Once the drugs have been metabolized, the individual will return to their normal state.

It is only when the cause of the excited delirium is mental illness that the antipsychotic medication is medically warranted. These individuals usually develop their excited delirium as a result of noncompliance with medication. For antipsychotic medication to be effective, a number of hours or days has to pass. If given initially at admission, by the time the antipsychotic medication would become effective, the patient might already be dead from excited delirium syndrome.

If the patient goes into cardiopulmonary arrest in the emergency room, in view of the prior discussion in this chapter on epinephrine, it would be advisable to use vasopressin for resuscitation.[24,25]

REFERENCES

1. O'Halloran, R.L. and Frank, J.G. Asphyxial death during prone restraint position revisited: a report of 21 cases. *Am. J. Forensic Med. Pathol.* 21(1):39–52, 2000.

2. Stratton, S.J., Rogers, C., Brickett, K., and Gruzinski, G. Factors associated with sudden death of individuals requiring restraint for excited delirium. *Am. J. Emerg. Med.* 19(3):187–191, 2001.

3. Chan, T.C., Vilke, G.N., Neuman, T., and Clausen, J.L. Restraint position and positional asphyxia. *Ann. Emerg. Med.* 30:578–586, 1997.

4. Chan, T.C., Neuman, T., Clausen, J., Eisele, J., and Vilke, G.M. Weight force during prone restraint and respiratory function. *Am. J. Forensic Med. Pathol.* 25:185–189, 2004.

5. Citrome, L. and Volavka, J. Violent patients in the emergency setting. *Psychiatr. Clin. North Am.* 22(4):789–801, 1999.

6. Grob, G.N. Mental health policy in America: myths and realities. *Health Affairs* 11(3):7–22, 1992.

7. Cancro, R. The introduction of neuroleptics: a psychiatric revolution. *Psychiatr. Serv.* 51(3):333–335, 2000.

8. Lieberman, J.A., Golden, R., Stroup, S., and McEnvoy, J. Drugs of the psycho-pharmacological revolution in clinical psychiatry. *Psychiatr. Serv.* 51(10) 1254–1258, 2000.

9. Wendkos, M.H. *Sudden Death and Psychiatric Illness.* SP Medical & Scientific Books, New York, 1979.

10. Brice, J.H., Pirrallo, R.G., Racht, E., Zachariah, B.S., and Krohmer, J. Management of the violent patient. *Prehosp. Emerg. Care* 7(1):48–55, 2002.

11. Tardiff, K. The current state of psychiatry in the treatment of violent patients. *Arch. Gen. Psychiatr.* 49(6):493–499, 1992.

12. Blumenreich, P., Lippmann, S., and Bacani-Oropilla, T. Violent patients. Are you prepared to deal with them? *Postgrad. Med.* 90(2):201–206, 1991.

13. Owen, C., Tarantello, C., Jones, M., and Tennant, C. Violence and aggression in psychiatric units. *Psychiatr. Serv.* 49(11):1452–1457, 1998.

14. Thompson, G.J. Verbal Judo for Police (Video Tape), Auburn, New York, 2000.

15. Ross, D.L. Factors associated with excited delirium deaths in police custody. *Mod. Pathol.* 11(11):1127–1137, 1998.

16. Dimsdale, J.E., Hartley, G.T., Guiney, T., Ruskin, J.N., and Greenblatt, D. Post-exercise peril: plasma catecholamines and exercise. *J. Am. Med. Assoc.* 251:630–632, 1984.

17. Glassman, A.H. and Bigger, J.T., Jr. Antipsychotic drugs: prolonged QTc interval, torsade de pointes, and sudden death. *Am. J. Psychiatr.* 158(11):1774–1782, 2001.

18. Herxheimer, A. Arrhythmias and sudden death in patients taking antipsychotic drugs. *Br. Med. J.* 325:1253–1254, 2002.

19. Fayek, M., Kingsbury, S.J., Zada, J., and Simpson, G.M. Psychopharmacology: cardiac effects of antipsychotic medications. *Psychiatr. Serv.* 52:607–609, 2001.

20. Witchel, H., Hancox, J.C., and Nutt, D.J. Psychotropic drugs, cardiac arrhythmia, and sudden death. *J. Clin. Psychopharmacol.* 23(1):58–77, 2003.

21. Hassaballa, H.A. and Balk, R.A. Torsade de pointes associated with the administration of intravenous haloperidol: a review of the literature and practical guidelines for use. *Expert Opin. Drug Saf.* 2(6):543–547, 2003.

22. Roden, D.M. Drug-induced prolongation of the QT interval. *N. Engl. J. Med.* 350(10):1013–1022, 2004.

23. Citrome, L. and Green, L. The dangerous agitated patient. What to do right now. *Postgrad. Med.* 87(2):231–236, 1990.

24. McIntyre, K.M. Vasopressin in asystolic cardiac arrest. *N. Engl. J. Med.* 350(2):179–181, 2004.

25. Wenzel, V., Krismer, A.C., Arntz, H.R., Sitter, H., Stadlbauer, K.H., and Lindner, K.H. European Resuscitation Council Vasopressor during Cardiopulmonary Resuscitation Study Group. A comparison of vasopressin and epinephrine for out-of-hospital cardiopulmonary resuscitation. *N. Engl. J. Med.* 350(2):105–113, 2004.

26. Tintinalli, J.E. and McCoy, M. Violent patients and the prehospital provider. Erratum appears in *Ann. Emerg. Med.* 22(8):1276–1279, 1993.

27. Citrome, L. Atypical antipsychotics for acute agitation. New intramuscular options offer advantages. *Postgrad. Med.* 112(6):85–88, 94–96, 2002.

28. Binder, R.L. and McNiel, D.E. Emergency psychiatry: contemporary practices in managing acutely violent patients in 20 psychiatric emergency rooms. *Psychiatr. Serv.* 50:1553–1554, 1999.

10

SUDDEN DEATH OF THE PSYCHIATRIC PATIENT IN MENTAL HEALTH FACILITIES

INTRODUCTION

The sudden death of psychiatric patients in mental institutions during states of excited delirium and violent behavior is not a new phenomenon. The medical literature on this syndrome in the United States describes these deaths as early as the mid-1800s.[1] This syndrome continues to occur and to be misunderstood by nursing and medical staff. Because of this, effective preventive strategies are not at present utilized.

Changes in psychiatric care have influenced the frequency and clinical presentation of deaths during excited delirium. Historically, care of the mentally ill client occurred in hospital-based facilities. This care was provided principally by nursing staff and was primarily custodial. Beginning in the late 1940s, detractors of mental hospitals began a campaign to replace them with community-based outpatient treatment facilities.[2] This campaign was aided by the introduction in the 1950s of psychotropic drugs for the treatment of severe mental disease.[3,4] This led to the widespread release of formerly institutionalized patients into the community. Community-based facilities were intended to provide comprehensive care focused on prevention and rehabilitation. Unfortunately, this proposed outpatient care was never adequately funded. Present-day communities now contain large numbers of mentally ill individuals who have little community mental health care. Medications that were previously prescribed to reduce psychosis in patients while being treated in hospital-based mental health facilities are no longer taken upon release into the community. Because of this, most deaths of mentally ill patients due to excited delirium syndrome occur outside mental health facilities, involve individuals who have discontinued their medications and/or are using alcohol or illegal stimulants such as cocaine, and take place while being arrested by police officers.

While less common, deaths due to excited delirium syndrome still occur in mental health facilities. These deaths are of the acute form rather than the chronic form seen in the 19th and early 20th centuries. Use of psychotropic drugs appears to be linked to a number of these excited delirium syndrome deaths. It should be understood, however, that any patient, at any time, for a variety of reasons, can develop excited delirium. Excited delirium can escalate to states of extreme violence requiring calling a code for restraint. It is the excited delirium, combined with a struggle against restraint, that precipitates sudden death due to excited delirium syndrome.

The role of the psychiatric nurse in preventing death from excited delirium syndrome cannot be underestimated. Psychiatric nursing emerged as a specialty in the United States at the McLean Psychiatric Asylum in 1882.[5] Then as today, the day-to-day care of patients with endogenous mental illness in mental health facilities was provided principally by nursing staff. Nursing staffs are the individuals who primarily respond to incidents of violence of mentally ill patients as well as represent the major targets of assaults by patients.[6] While excited delirium by mentally ill patients is not an uncommon event for nursing staff, sudden death due to excited delirium syndrome is. Physicians are rarely involved during the acute phases of excited delirium when death may occur. The exception to this is in emergency hospital settings. Therefore, this chapter's main focus is on prevention of death due to excited delirium syndrome by nursing personnel.

Identifying patients at high risk for excited delirium syndrome is the *first step* toward death prevention. Once at-risk individuals are identified, preventive procedures intended to alter actions that initiate the sequence of events culminating in death can be implemented. All medical facilities faced with violent individuals, whether the cause of this aggression and violence is drug related or psychological, should incorporate these preventive strategies for excited delirium syndrome into their occupational and safety training policies on the management of violence and aggression.

A new screening tool for early risk assessment for excited delirium syndrome is presented in this chapter (Table 10.1). This tool can be utilized during the admission of patients and made part of the medical record. This assessment screening tool is derived from current and historical reports of sudden death in psychiatric patients, as well as the experience of one of the authors (T.G.D.) working with acutely violent patients suffering from a variety of mental illnesses. This author has participated in and been responsible for calling codes for physical and chemical restraint procedures for extreme violent behavior.

Recommendations addressing preventive care measures are provided in an attempt to prevent future deaths from excited delirium syndrome. It is hoped that these proposed nursing strategies will be incorporated into safety training protocols and unit care policies for psychiatric health facilities that treat and care for the mentally ill client.

One other point should be mentioned. At the present time, we do not know how many individuals die of excited delirium syndrome. This includes cases due to use of illicit drugs as well as those associated with endogenous mental illness; cases of dying in institutions or in the community. There should be established a nationwide data bank for all deaths due to excited delirium syndrome. Centralizing such data will provide information on the frequency of these deaths; factors precipitating them; and effective medical and behavioral procedures and techniques that can be used to prevent them.

IDENTIFYING PATIENTS SUSCEPTIBLE TO EXCITED DELIRIUM SYNDROME

Preventing deaths due to excited delirium syndrome in psychiatric facilities requires the *early identification of high-risk patients.* This necessitates understanding the physiological mechanisms causing sudden death, identifying key behavioral characteristics that signal its onset, and instituting measures to prevent its occurrence.

Assessing those patients who are at high risk for excited delirium syndrome can be accomplished during admission and made part of the patient's record. Although any patient may die suddenly during a code for violent behavior, there is a particular subgroup of mentally ill patients who are at extreme high risk for sudden death due to excited delirium syndrome. Documentation of these individuals in the medical records provides continuity of care from admission to inpatient care. This early identification of potential cases of excited delirium syndrome can signal staff of the high risk potential for sudden death if a code is required and a physical struggle occurs.

As a tool for patient care, accurate nursing diagnoses have always been of fundamental importance. Assessment for prevention of sudden death due to excited delirium syndrome can be another measure of patient care. Thus, a "nursing diagnosis" might be *"Potential for sudden death due to excited delirium syndrome: as evidenced by a history of endogenous mental disease with past violent behavior with a history of illicit drug or alcohol use."*

Predictive Characteristics of Violent and Aggressive Patients

Violence in health-care settings is a complex problem with numerous antecedents. Characteristics of violent patients are not unique to a particular group, but can originate from a variety of types of patients suffering from complex health and social issues.[7,8] The results of violent behavior by patients can be lethal to themselves, medical personnel, or other patients. These incidents are a frequent event with the target of this violence primarily directed toward nursing staff.[6, 9–11]

In cases of excited delirium syndrome, extreme violent behavior, requiring staff intervention, typically precedes death. A violent "struggle" for control of the patient then occurs. It is the time prior to the struggle that death prevention for excited delirium syndrome must focus its efforts. Intervention at this time may prevent death.

Although there have been no large studies of patients with excited delirium attempting to determine the different levels of aggression and how and when nursing staff should intervene, there have been studies of violence in the general health-care setting. Haber et al.[12] studied aggressive behavior in a Veterans Affairs medical center, many of whose patients had long histories of chronic mental illness. They identified three sets of behavior that appeared to reflect different levels of aggression. They referred to these as scales and named them *Precursor, Defensive*, and *Acting Out.*

The Precursor Scale described such behavior as:

> Easily excited, constantly in motion, inappropriate affect, delusional, hyperactive, ideas of persecution, disorganized thinking, confused, disoriented, angry, trembling angry, negative, appears tense, hyperactive, loud, irritable, constantly in motion.[12]

The intermediate level of aggressive behavior was the Defensive Scale. Behavior mentioned included:

> Shouting angrily, hostile, clenched fists, curses viciously, vicious insults, impulsively threatening violence, threatening violence deliberately or repeatedly, slams door angrily, temper outbursts, vicious insults, curses viciously.[12]

The Acting Out Scale constituted the most serious behavior:

> Grabbing others, kicking, scratching, pushing, pulling hair, tears clothes, throws objects dangerously, breaks objects, throws self

on floor, swinging at others, striking out, bangs head, pulls out hair, hits self without injury.[12]

The importance of this research in sudden death prevention for excited delirium syndrome is in the ranking of precursor behaviors indicative of aggression and violence. Monitoring patients at risk for excited delirium syndrome must include early identification of behaviors predictive of violent activity. Once identified, there should be an immediate therapeutic intervention to reduce escalating anger and aggression. The staff surveyed in this study identified the use of physical intervention as indicated only when the behavior falls in the Acting Out Scale and the Defensive Scale.[12] However, it is within the Precursor Scale that death prevention from excited delirium syndrome must be addressed. The initial use of verbal de-escalation as well as the offering of sedative mediations to reduce agitation must begin at the Precursor Scale.

Behaviors identified by medical staff who have witnessed deaths due to excited delirium syndrome include:[12]

Extreme agitation
Hyperactivity
Extreme irritability
Defiance
Loud and pressured speech
Anger
Suspiciousness
Bullying others
Screaming, swearing, shouting at others
Delusions and/or hallucination (delusions are usually of a paranoid type)
Disorganized thinking
Refusal to yield to any verbal intervention
Refusal to eat or sleep
Verbal threats of violence
Acting out behaviors, i.e., swinging at others, attacking others
Breaking and throwing objects
Violent behavior or a history of violent behavior
Aggressive and assaultive behavior

Mental Illness

Excited delirium syndrome is identified almost exclusively with two mental illnesses: schizophrenia with paranoid features and the mood disorder of mania (bipolar disease). The inherent nature of these mental illnesses often involves "bizarre" behaviors such as described and witnessed in sudden death due to excited delirium syndrome.

The thought content of schizophrenic individuals is disrupted. Paranoid delusions with suspicions of other people are often present during a psychotic break with reality. These delusions will create tremendous fear and agitation that may result in violent behavior. Hallucinations may be present. Patients will often describe "bugs crawling over them" or they see the "devil." They may tell you that they hear "God" or the "devil" speaking to them telling them to do things. These hallucinations can be very dangerous if a health worker or another patient is the object of their anger or fear.

With extreme manic behavior, there is impairment of concentration with a loss of social inhibitions. Behavior may be argumentative, restless, and irritable. Psychotic features may be present. Because of the excessive expansiveness of mood during periods of extreme mania, these individuals may be viewed as "bizarre" by others. Their behavior may appear dramatic and theatrical with rapid speech.[13] Thus, both schizophrenia and bipolar disease can be considered risk factors for excited delirium syndrome.

Miscellaneous Characteristics of Excited Delirium Syndrome

Nursing personnel must recognize not only these two factors but others and incorporate them into a risk assessment scale for each patient. Additional characteristics of high-risk patients are as follows:

- A prior episode of excited delirium
- Violent and aggressive behavior or a prior history of these behaviors
- Behavior requiring physical intervention by staff
- Use of stimulants such as cocaine and methamphetamine
- Use of medication that increases release or blocks reuptake of norepinephrine
- Medications that cause prolongation of the QT interval, e.g., antipsychotics, antidepressants
- History of a natural disease that may contribute to sudden death, i.e., cardiac disease, asthma, alcoholism

Age is not an identifying factor, as these deaths can occur in the young as well as the old. Table 10.1 provides a tool to screen patients in terms of their potential to develop excited delirium syndrome. A value of 0 to 8 indicates low risk; 10 to 13 medium risk; and 15 and higher a high risk for excited delirium syndrome.

Table 10.1 Assessment of the Psychiatric Patient for Risk of Excited Delirium Syndrome

1. Diagnosis of schizophrenia and other psychotic disorders	5 points ( )
2. Past history of violent behavior requiring physical restraint	5 points ( )
3. History of abuse of stimulants (e.g., cocaine, methamphetamine, PCP)	5 points ( )
4. History of natural disease possessing life-threatening potential (cardiovascular diseases; central nervous system disorders, e.g., epilepsy; pulmonary disorders, e.g., asthma, chronic obstructive pulmonary disease)	1 point ( )
5. Alcoholism	1 point ( )
6. Use of cardiotoxic medications (e.g., tricyclic antidepressants)	1 point ( )

A value of 0 to 8 indicates low risk; 10 to 13 medium risk; and 15 and higher a high risk for excited delirium syndrome.

Note: If there is a history that the patient required cardiopulmonary resuscitation for any prior condition involving cardiac, pulmonary or psychiatric states, a struggle and physical restraint should be avoided. Medical or other related personnel should be instructed in the use of alternative methods to be employed to reduce escalating violent behavior that could result in a need to use physical restraint.

PREVENTING SUDDEN DEATH FROM EXCITED DELIRIUM SYNDROME

Observation in Sudden Death Prevention

> In dwelling upon the vital importance of sound observation, it must never be lost sight of what observation is for. It is not for the sake of piling up miscellaneous information or curious facts, but for the sake of saving life and increasing health and comfort.
>
> **— Florence Nightingale 1860**
> (from F. Nightingale, *Notes on Nursing*)

The importance of experienced and trained psychiatric nursing personnel must be mentioned early on in this discussion of death prevention strategies for excited delirium syndrome. Although research provides a framework for practice, it cannot replace experience and training in behavioral management of violent patients. The art of *"observation"* and having a *skilled "sense"* of a patient's behavior cannot be overlooked. This "skilled sense" is also mentioned by law enforcement officers when they are following leads that do not appear to be connected at first glance.

Experienced psychiatric nursing staff that have worked with patients with a variety of mental, physical, and social health-related illnesses will often explain that they first "sensed" something different in the patient's behavior, mood, or affect prior to an incident of violent behavior. It is this unique ability to be able to perceive the quiet changes or differences in an individual's behavior, mood, or affect that will often signal the precursors to violent behavior by a patient. These changes will often go unrecognized by the inexperienced, untrained health-care professional. This "sensed change" is not something that can be learned from studying research on violence prevention, but is related to training and experience in working with psychiatric patients.

The untrained and/or inexperienced staff member often judges the characteristic quality of mood solely by the patient's affect, neglecting to question patients about their feelings. Questioning the patients about "feelings" often provides a better insight into a patient's actual mood status. "The dimensions of mood, i.e., quality, stability, reactivity, intensity, and duration cannot be determined solely by observation of affect." Determining changes in mood must include frequent questioning of the patient as to his or her "feelings."[14]

Changes in a patient's behavior, mood, or affect can occur from moment to moment, or day to day. Discerning these changes by experienced medical personnel members who have been exposed to violent behavior is critical in sudden death preventive strategies for excited delirium syndrome.

Attempting to De-Escalate the Situation

Prevention of excited delirium syndrome–related deaths requires preventing the use of physical restraint and the struggle associated with it, in other words, defusing the situation so that it is not necessary to call a code. As initial attempts at de-escalation by verbal intervention are usually made by the primary nurse, who often has no or minimal support, this may result in a code being called too quickly. The patient is then confronted with five to six personnel. The involvement of too many staff members may create an environment that is unsettling and confusing to the patient. Too many demand statements directed toward patients who are unable to process their thoughts or control their emotions at this initial stage of aggression is detrimental and potentially harmful to the process of de-escalation.

Ideally, more than one skilled professional should be attending a patient. Limiting the staff to two individuals, with one addressing the agitated individual and the other preparing the environment for further escalation should it be necessary, is one possibility. Having two individuals working with the patient provides for a more controlled scene. There is less mental confusion and fear by patients when only one person confronts him or her vs. a six-person team. The staff of two is not confused as to who does what in these situations.

This is not to say that having a "team approach" to potentially violent patients is not preferable. Having a team approach, however, requires members of the team to be trained in their roles in de-escalation of a violent patient. If initial attempts at de-escalation by the primary staff member fail, another team member can assume the primary role with the initial member at standby if further escalation of violence becomes evident. The second member of the team then assumes the role of the primary and once again attempts to "verbally intervene with the patient." The rationale for this changing of roles is that often the primary nursing staff member is identified by the patient as a target for aggression. Having another staff member address the patient after the primary allows the patient to feel that he or she is being understood. While one member of the team talks to the patient another can prepare medication for injection while the others are "securing" the environment by removing other patients, objects, or other noxious stimuli that might contribute to the violent incident. The advantage of having a team of six members for rapid control of the patient is that if physical restrain has to be used, the time of the struggle can be reduced.

When attempting de-escalation by verbal intervention, it is vitally important that staff members display a calm and nonthreatening behavior toward the patient. No rapid movements toward the patient should be attempted. The sound of the primary team member's voice should be firm but not assertive, calm but not timid, direct, and clearly understandable. Verbal requests must be simple and time must be allowed for the patient to respond as long as there is not imminent danger. While this seems both obvious and simple, it is often difficult to achieve in a very intense and fearful atmosphere. One of the authors (T.G.D.) has witnessed experienced psychiatric staff members confronting extremely aggressive and agitated patients with a rough and loud demeanor. Hands are gesturing wildly (this may be viewed by the patient as objects of an attack; therefore, one's hands should be at the side of the body with palms open) and the body language is confrontational. Statements are authoritative and demanding with little patience directed toward the patient. Being calm and nonthreatening becomes difficult in the face of extreme danger to self.

Statements directed in a nonthreatening manner that support the individual's own ability to maintain behavioral self-control are what is needed initially, e.g., expressing sincere belief statements offering to help the patient. This will reduce levels of anxiety and mistrust. A positive statements might be "we are here to help you," "how can I help you," "I see you may need my help," "I know we can help you calm down." These statements help establish rapport, provide a time period for the patient to regain behavioral control, as well as allowing the individual to express and vent his or her own internal dialogue and emotions. The information being expressed by the patients will aid in determining the next step in the process of de-escalation.

Individuals in a state of acute psychosis are not in control of reality. Therefore, statements expressed in an authoritative, forceful, or judgmental manner *will not help* to reduce aggression or the potential for violence. Initial verbal attempts to de-escalate a psychotic agitated patient must be limited to "supportive" statements. You are trying to "buy time" in attempts to get the patient to regain emotional control. Placing time restraints such as "right now" only will add to the anxiety of the patient. Initial intervention statements should include offering the patient medications that are familiar and will help reduce anxiety.

One should listen to the patient's explanation of the events, no matter how bizarre they seem, and provide emotional support by statements such as "I can see you are upset," "How can I be of help to you." Do not make promises unless you can keep them and do not lie. If you fail to keep a promise, the patient will remember and hold it against you the next time. The only time one should lie to a patient is when there is a situation requiring life and death decisions.

It is important to mention that staff must keep a safe distance from any psychotic and "bizarre" patient who appears extremely agitated. Violent assaultive behavior may occur rapidly and it is always necessary to have an avenue of escape. Psychotic agitated patients are very difficult and dangerous to deal with. Staff cannot expect them to cognitively interpret, rationalize, and respond to requests in a "normal" time or manner. Often, these patients harbor persecutory delusions and those delusions can and often do include staff. Providing oral medications for sedation of aggressive behaviors along with antipsychotic medications for breakthrough of psychotic features is required immediately. If sedation is not achieved by the offering of oral medications early in the development of agitation and aggression, the probability is likely that a code for physical restraint will be required.

Use of Physical Restraint

Physical restraint must be used with caution in cases of excited delirium. This fact cannot be stressed too much. Physical restraint is never to be used for behavioral management of patients but only when there is serious risk of harm to the staff, others, and the patient. The use of any type of physical restraint may initiate the "struggle" that engages the cascade of physiological responses culminating in sudden death due to excited delirium syndrome. Thus, use of restraint in cases of excited delirium must only be initiated with a clear understanding of the potential for sudden death that it carries with it.

If use of physical restraint is unavoidable, the use of approximately six individuals trained in approved physical restraint techniques is recommended. This is necessary to obtain rapid restraint, thus reducing the time of struggle, and the cascading physiological response mechanisms inherent in excited delirium syndrome. Four of the six will secure the extremities, one the trunk, and the sixth prepare and administer sedative medication.

Chemical Restraint

Chemical restraint, involving use of medications to sedate agitated individuals prior to, during, or immediately after a struggle, is customarily accomplished by the intramuscular route. The standard treatment for extreme agitation in emergency settings is often a combination of a benzodiazepine (most often lorazepam) in conjunction with an antipsychotic (most often haloperidol). The typical dose ranges for rapid sedation and control of the violent behavior are as follows: lorazepam, 0.5 to 2.0 mg every 1 to 6 hours; haloperidol, 5 to 10 mg.[15,16]

Unfortunately, most antipsychotic medications have side effects that make their use potentially dangerous in excited delirium situations. Haloperidol, the most commonly used antipsychotic used in treatment of excited delirium, like many antipsychotics, may cause prolongation of the QT interval.[17–21] Thus, the hyperadrenergic state present in excited delirium with its potential to produce cardiac arrhythmias may be compounded by the antipsychotic medications with their own potential for producing arrhythmias.

The need to administer any type of antipsychotic medications at any time during a code for excited delirium and/or extreme aggressive and agitated behavior should be reconsidered by medical personnel. The therapeutic benefits, reduction of psychotic features along with sedation, must be weighed against the potential for cardiac arrhythmia. Although customary as a first-line measure for acute psychosis or excited delirium, violent behavior in the psychiatric patient on a psychiatric unit does not usually occur from lack of antipsychotic medication that is given daily. Rather, situations on the unit such as staffing levels, patient mix, overcrowding, noise, lack of diversionary activities and family visits are the factors in precipitating excited delirium and violence. Additionally, the use of antipsychotic medications for a patient brought into an emergency hospital with no known history of mental illness can be potentially lethal. Rapid sedation can be achieved by administration of a benzodiazepine without the conjunctive use of an antipsychotic medication.

Rapid sedation is the most important procedure in preventing death from excited delirium syndrome once restraint is used. Benzodiazepines although absorbed readily following intramuscular administration do not provide the quickest method of sedation. The onset of action by the intramuscular route is 15 to 30 minutes with a peak effect in 1 hour. Rapid sedation by the intravenous route with a benzodiazepine is preferable. Onset of action is immediate. Intravenous administration when given must not be so rapid as to produce apnea or bradycardia.

The authors of this book have concluded that the *single most important factor* that determines if individuals experiencing excited delirium die is the violent physical exertion inherent in the *struggle*. This is true whether the excited delirium is due to drugs, mental illness, or a combination of both. Placing an individual in a *prone position* is not a critical element for most excited delirium syndrome deaths. During episodes of excited delirium, it is necessary to abort the struggle, not address the psychotic features of the episode. Avoiding "post-exercise peril" is the primary therapeutic objective in death prevention from excited delirium syndrome.

Post-Restraint

After restraining the patient, continual assessment of the individual's level of consciousness and breathing should be maintained with "face-to-face" observation by one member of the team. One should monitor the vital signs for signs of cardiac irregularities. The patient should be immediately sedated using medication free of possible cardiotoxic potential, e.g., benzodiazepines. Lorazepam is recommended.[15] The route of administration for extreme agitation should be intravenous not intramuscular. Because of the rapid nature of sudden death due to excited delirium syndrome, usually within minutes after a struggle occurs, it is extremely important to sedate the patient immediately.

The patient should be maintained in a sitting position for maximum breathing ability. If this position is not possible due to maintenance of physical control, an alternative position is "side-lying." Side-lying may in fact be the best position if the individual is very obese. Cardiac arrest almost invariably occurs shortly after the individual ceases to struggle regardless of the "position." There is no scientific proof that any position reduces the probability of death. Positioning is for the most part done for legal reasons, not medical.

Be prepared to provide oxygen, institute cardiopulmonary resuscitation, and summon the EMS for transport to an emergency room. If the facility is capable of administering advanced cardiac life support (ACLS), recent studies suggest use of vasopressin rather than epinephrine.[22,23]

OVERVIEW OF PREVENTIVE MEASURES

The following are *primary* death preventive strategies for excited delirium syndrome suggested for all health facilities that receive and treat violent patients:

Education

Provide in-service educational and training programs to nursing staff on causes of sudden death due to excited delirium. Thus, in-service program focus should be on:

- Excited delirium syndrome, facts and myths
- Physiological mechanisms of sudden death from excited delirium syndrome
- Identifying types of patients that potentially can present with excited delirium, i.e., history of mental health issues unique to this sudden death syndrome
- Identifying behavior presentation features of patients in excited delirium
- Developing guidelines and preventive measures to abort the need for use of restraints

Preparation

- Prepare a risk assessment screening tool for potentially violent patients
- Prepare an excited delirium syndrome risk assessment screening tool for patients when admitted for a psychiatric emergency or to a psychiatric unit
- Review and evaluate the patient's present and past medical and psychiatric history including medications
- Document and flag patient charts that present with known identified clinical precursors of sudden death due to excited delirium syndrome, i.e., history of schizophrenia or bipolar disorder, illicit drug use
- Have a "team plan" to prevent the need for a code for physical restraint
- Develop clinical standards for emergency psychiatric care procedures for the prevention and management of behavioral emergencies — these procedures should be researched and evidence-based and supported by mental health and nursing research; stress should be on preventing the need for any type of physical "struggle" with the patient

A complete evaluation of the patient's present and past medical and psychiatric history should be conducted. This should include the reason for voluntary or involuntary admission. Involuntary admissions to psychiatric or emergency facilities are often related to violent or potentially violent behavior, thus the risk for excited delirium syndrome is greater.[11,15] Any history of prior violence, use of weapons, alcohol and/or illicit drug abuse, should be flagged and highlighted. These factors have been identified as important risk factors for future episodes of violent behavior.[6,7,15,16] Additionally, those individuals on antipsychotic medications that cause prolongation of the QT interval are more susceptible to a fatal cardiac arrhythmia.

Significance of a Medical History in Cases of Excited Delirium Syndrome

Psychiatric nursing care is primarily focused on the stabilization of maladaptive behaviors and affective disorders. Nursing intervention skills are concerned with assessing inappropriate responses, dispensing psychotropic medications, and monitoring their side effects. Daily physical assessment of a patient's total health status, especially cardiovascular and respiratory, is often not done. The psychiatric nursing staff must not lose sight of the necessity to assess for any disease state that can contribute to the sudden death of their patients. An alteration in cardiac status may occur due to other health conditions or the long-term use of psychotropic medications. These alterations may be missed without regular physical assessment. This lack of assessment may prove to be a fatal factor if a code for physical restraint occurs.

Part of the total patient assessment should include the medications the patient is taking and their potential for cardiac toxicity. Many antipsychotic drugs and antidepressants currently prescribed produce cardiac irregularities by prolongation of the QT interval.[20,24] Drug-induced prolongation of the QT interval may progress to torsade de pointes, which in turn results in ventricular fibrillation.[24] Following are some commonly used antipsychotic drugs that cause this fatal form of cardiac arrhythmia:

Chlorpromazine (Thorazine)
Haloperidol (Haldol)
Mesoridazine (Serentil)
Thioridazine (Mellaril)
Pimozide

Because many psychotropic medications have potentially fatal side effects related to prolongation of the QT interval, routine electrocardiograms are advisable. A baseline electrocardiogram should be completed on admission and repeated on a weekly basis as new medications are prescribed and titrated to the patient. With long-term-care patients, where medication prescription is stable, electrocardiograms may be performed on a quarterly basis as long as physical assessments are negative. In a patient with underlying cardiac disease, it may be advisable to perform routine electrocardiograms more frequently.

Additional risk factors for sudden cardiac arrest are as follows:[24]

Hypokalemia
Bradycardia
Congestive heart failure
Baseline QT prolongation
Subclinical long QT syndrome
Severe hypomagnesemia
Recent conversion from atrial fibrillation, especially with a QT-prolonging drug

The importance of these additional clinical risk factors in preventing death from excited delirium syndrome in the psychiatric patient is that they increase the probability for sudden death to occur during a code for physical restraint.

Management of Aggression and Prevention of Violence within the Psychiatric Community

Because of the problem of aggression and violent behavior in the health-care setting, the U.S. Office of Safety and Health Administration (OSHA) has recommended guidelines for all health-care facilities in providing education on these issues. Several agencies have developed programs directed to this problem. Morrison and Love[25] evaluated four training programs that addressed the management of aggression and prevention of violence within the psychiatric community. They researched the therapeutic effectiveness of these programs based on professional and clinical principles of psychiatric care. These programs were the Mandt System, the Nonviolent Crises Intervention (NCI) Program, Professional Assault Response Training 2000 (PART 2000), and Therapeutic Options (TO) programs. Several areas within these programs were evaluated: content of subject, feasibility, psychological comfort of staff, effectiveness, and cost of training. Of the programs evaluated, the TO and PART scored the highest. What is of interest is that none of these programs incorporated nursing research to support the program. Only PART 2000 attempts to introduce and incorporate treatment planning with the management of aggressive behavior, and is concerned with how the management of an aggressive behavior program fits into the overall treatment plan. Only the TO program recognizes the importance of a therapeutic relationship between patient and staff.

Several criticisms of the programs are mentioned in the article: most assume that patients are cooperating when in actuality they are not; team techniques are not sufficiently covered; and, last, there is insufficient evaluation of improvement data.[25] Thus, at present, there is no standard program for preventative strategies for violence and aggressive behavior management. The programs currently utilized have defects and do not incorporate nursing research. A program should be developed correcting the deficiencies in the present programs and utilizing clinically sound, nursing research-based preventative strategies.

CONCLUSION

It is important to mention at this time that the authors do not contend that there has not been or will not be cases of wrongful death due to actions of the medical staff. However, the use of physical and chemical restraint by trained medical personnel does not cause the death of patients in and of itself in most cases.

Any medical professional who has ever been involved in a code to "take down" a patient knows that this action is not entered into lightly or without forethought regarding the dangers inherent in this act. The responders to a code assume moral, professional, ethical, and legal responsibilities.[26] It is not, however, only the patient's legal rights and physical being that is in immediate danger during an episode of excited delirium; it is also those of the health-care professionals who have been designated to care for them.

It is absurd to believe that one nurse, usually female, can provide full care to multiple patients with histories of serious violent psychotic behaviors and yet, somehow, not have a need to call a code. Many critics of nursing staff calling codes, including physicians, have no daily experience caring for mentally ill patients. After having reviewed numerous articles by various governmental and private oversight agencies, it is apparent that many of these individuals have a totally unrealistic perception of mental health facilities, mentally ill patients, and their potential for violence. The reality faced by the community of clinical psychiatric nurses today is quite a different one from that envisioned by critics. Very few individuals go to work wondering if they might be attacked or stabbed during their workday, but violence against nurses is common in psychiatric facilities nationwide.[27] Little is done to protect them from violent assault.[28]

Not only are psychiatric nurses at high risk for physical violence, but they also have little means of protection when a rapidly escalating violent episode occurs on the unit. Their only resource is to call a code for help. Police and emergency personnel have other means of protecting themselves from harm when presented with violent individuals. Police often work in pairs and can use handcuffs, pepper spray, Tasers, batons, and even guns to protect themselves. Emergency personnel usually have support personnel close by and are never alone when having to protect themselves, the patient, and others from harm. They are equipped to administer rapid-acting medications that quickly sedate individuals if necessary.

Individuals who have never been involved in a code for violent behavior cannot appreciate the level of strength that even an adolescent patient exerts, not to mention a 200-lb adult male patient. This "reality" of the situation faced by psychiatric nurses nationwide is usually never mentioned in articles criticizing nursing personnel dealing with mentally ill patients.

Although nursing staff members are often the victims of violence, nursing schools' educational programs fail to adequately address how to identify precursor behaviors of violence, the management of aggressive and violent patients, or prevention of violence by the patients they serve.[29]

Hospital- and emergency-based facilities have the advantage of being able to utilize rapid intravenous sedative medications. The majority of nonhospital-based psychiatric facilities utilize oral or intramuscular antipsychotic and sedative medications. The peak onset of these medications is too long to be effective in reducing aggression. Sudden death occur immediately to minutes "after" the struggle ceases. The usual protocol for administering intramuscular sedatives/antipsychotic medication in psychiatric facilities is if the patient *refuses* oral administration or *after* the individual has been restrained. This administration of medication is often too late to prevent sudden death due to excited delirium syndrome. Rapid sedation is needed and only intravenous medication would be beneficial in these cases.

Every time psychiatric personnel members call a code for a violent psychiatric patient, they face the potential that death may occur. If this occurs, they are often blamed for inappropriate conduct with claims of positional asphyxia as the cause of death. The psychiatric staff does have the advantage over police, EMS, and emergency room staff of observing day-to-day and moment-to-moment changes in patient behavior signaling the potential for violent occurrences. They can act early on with psychological, verbal, and behavior techniques to prevent violence on their units. Unfortunately, many psychiatric units are understaffed and the personnel is for the most part unaware of the excited delirium syndrome. Thus, the staff's advantage is often more theoretical than actual. If staffing is sufficient, the nursing personnel can detect the signs of an impending episode of excited delirium and take preventive measures. The use of sedative medications should become the first intervention after initial verbal techniques fail to help the patient gain self-control. Their use may prevent the struggle that precedes death from excited delirium syndrome and, hopefully, the death.

REFERENCES

1. Bell, L.V. On a form of disease resembling some advanced stages of mania and fever. *Am. J. Insanity* 6:97–127, 1849.

2. Grob, G.N. Mental health policy in America: myths and realities. *Health Affairs* 11(3):7–22, 1992.

3. Cancro, R. The introduction of neuroleptics: a psychiatric revolution. *Psychiatr. Serv.* 51(3):333–335, 2000.

4. Lieberman, J.A., Golden, R., Stroup, S., and McEnvoy, J. Drugs of the psycho-pharmacological revolution in clinical psychiatry. *Psychiatr. Serv.* 51(10):1254–1258, 2000.

5. DeSalvo Rankin, E.A. Psychiatric/mental health nursing. *Nurs. Clin. North Am.* 21(3):381–386, 1986.

6. Owen, C., Tarantello, C., Jones, M., and Tennant. C. Violence and aggression in psychiatric units. *Psychiatr. Serv.* 49(11):1452–1457, 1998.

7. Tardiff, K. The current state of psychiatry in the treatment of violent patients. *Arch. Gen. Psychiatr.* 49(6):493–499, 1992.

8. Mason, T. and Chandley, M. *Management of Violence and Aggression. A Manual for Nurses and Health Care Workers.* Churchill Livingstone, London, 1999.

9. Lipscomb, J.A. and Love, C.C. Violence toward health care workers: an emerging occupational hazard. *AAOHN J.* 40(5):219–228, 1992.

10. Rippon, T.J. Aggression and violence in health care professions. *J. Adv. Nurs.* 31(2):452–460, 2000.

11. Blumenreich, P., Lippmann, S., and Bacani-Oropilla, T. Violent patients. Are you prepared to deal with them? *Postgrad. Med.* 90(2):201–206, 1991.

12. Haber, L.C., Fagan-Pryor, E.C., and Allen, M. Comparison of registered nurses' and nursing assistants' choices of intervention for aggressive behaviors. *Iss. Mental Health Nurs.* 18(2):113–124, 1997.

13. American Psychiatric Association. *Diagnostic and Statistical Manual of Mental Disorders,* 4th ed. Text Rev. American Psychiatric Association, Washington, D.C., 2000.

14. Othmer, E. and Othmer, S.C. *The Clinical Interview Using DSM-IV. Vol. 1: Fundamentals.* American Psych. Press, 1994.

15. Citrome, L. and Volavka, J. Violent patients in the emergency setting. *Psychiatr. Clin. North Am.* 22(4):789–801, 1999.

16. Brice, J.H., Pirrallo, R.G., Racht, E., Zachariah, B.S., and Krohmer, J. Management of the violent patient. *Prehosp. Emerg. Care* 7(1):48–55, 2002.

17. Glassman, A.H. and Bigger, J.T., Jr. Antipsychotic drugs: prolonged QTc interval, torsade de pointes, and sudden death. *Am. J. Psychiatr.* 158(11):1774–1782, 2001.

18. Herxheimer, A. Arrhythmias and sudden death in patients taking antipsychotic drugs. *Br. Med. J.* 325:1253–1254, 2002.

19. Fayek, M., Kingsbury, S.J., Zada, J., and Simpson, G.M. Psychopharmacology: cardiac effects of antipsychotic medications. *Psychiatr. Serv.* 52:607–609, 2001.

20. Witchel, H., Hancox, J.C., and Nutt, D.J. Psychotropic drugs, cardiac arrhythmia, and sudden death. *J. Clin. Psychopharmacol.* 23(1):58–77, 2003.

21. Hassaballa, H.A. and Balk, R.A. Torsade de pointes associated with the administration of intravenous haloperidol: a review of the literature and practical guidelines for use. *Expert Opin. Drug Saf.* 2(6):543–547, 2003.

22. McIntyre, K.M. Vasopressin in asystolic cardiac arrest. *N. Engl. J. Med.* 350(2):179–181, 2004.

23. Wenzel, V., Krismer, A.C., Arntz, H.R., Sitter, H., Stadlbauer, K.H., and Lindner, K.H. European Resuscitation Council Vasopressor during Cardiopulmonary Resuscitation Study Group. A comparison of vasopressin and epinephrine for out-of-hospital cardiopulmonary resuscitation. *N. Engl. J. Med.* 350(2):105–113, 2004.

24. Roden, D.M. Drug-induced prolongation of the QT interval. *N. Engl. J. Med.* 350(10):1013–1022, 2004.

25. Morrison, E.F. and Love, C.C. An evaluation of four programs for the management of aggression in psychiatric settings. *Arch. Psychiatr. Nurs.* 17(4):146–155, 2003.

26. Austin, W. Relational ethics in forensic psychiatric settings. *J. Psychosoc. Nurs. Mental Health Serv.* 39(9):12–17, 2001.

27. Lam, J.N., McNiel, D.E., and Binder, R.L. The relationship between patients' gender and violence leading to staff injuries. *Psychiatr. Serv.* 51(9):1167–1170, 2000.

28. Grace, P.J., Fry, S.T., and Schultz, G.S. Ethics and human rights issues experienced by psychiatric-mental health and substance abuse registered nurses. *J. Am. Psychiatr. Nurs. Assoc.* 9(1): 17–23, 2003.

29. Love, C.C. and Elliot, J.D. Violence in forensic psychiatric settings: roadblocks to effective monitoring and prevention. *On the Edge (IAFN newsl.).* 8(2), 2002.

INDEX

135